A MINORITY OF ONE

First published May 1988

ISBN 0 85245 207 1

Cover design and typography by Jack Slade
Back cover photograph by Riccardo Gill

Printed in Great Britain in 10/12 Palatino and 11/12
Palatino italic
by Headley Brothers Ltd., The Invicta Press, Ashford,
Kent and London

SWARTHMORE LECTURE 1988

A MINORITY
OF
ONE
a journey
with Friends

by Harvey Gillman

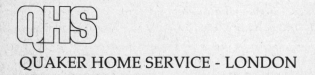

QUAKER HOME SERVICE - LONDON

Permissions

The author and Quaker Home Service gladly make
acknowledgement to the following writers and
publishers to reprint from copyright sources:
Prentice-Hall Inc for the extract from *Stigma* by
Erving Goffman; Bear & Company for the extract
from *Meditations with Hildegard of Bingen* by
Gabriele Uhlein (© 1983); George Borchardt Inc and
Penguin Books Ltd for the extract from *Souls on Fire*
by Elie Wiesel (© 1972 by Elie Wiesel); Chatto &
Windus for the extract from *View from Christopher
Street* edited by M. Denneny; Clarkson N. Potter Inc
for the extract from *The Annotated Alice* introduced
by Martin Gardner; A. R. Mowbray & Co Ltd for the
extract from *Meditation on a Theme* by Anthony
Bloom; Hugh McGregor Ross for the extract from
The Gospel of Thomas presented by Hugh McGregor
Ross; Oxford University Press for the extract from
Gaia: A New Look at Life on Earth by James Lovelock
(© 1982); Routledge & Kegan Paul for the extract
from *Psychological Reflections* edited by Joland
Jacobi; Thank You Music Ltd for the words of *Please
Break This Bread Lord* by Jodi Page Clark. Extracts
from *Seeds of Contemplation* by Thomas Merton is
used by permission of the publisher Anthony
Clarke, Wheathampstead, England.

Preface

The Swarthmore Lectureship was established by the Woodbrooke Extension Committee at a meeting held December 9th, 1907: the minute of the Committee providing for an 'an annual lecture on some subject relating to the message and work of the Society of Friends'. The name Swarthmore was chosen in memory of the home of Margaret Fox, which was always open to the earnest seeker after Truth, and from which loving words of sympathy and substantial material help were sent to fellow workers.

The lectureship has a twofold purpose: first, to interpret to the members of the Society of Friends their message and mission; and secondly, to bring before the public the spirit, the aims and fundamental principles of Friends. The lecturer alone is responsible for any opinions expressed.

The lectureship provides both for the publication of a book and for the delivery of a lecture, the latter usually at the time of assembly of London Yearly Meeting of the Society of Friends. A lecture related to the present book was delivered at Friends House, Euston Road, London, on the evening of May 28th, 1988.

Contents

To my parents, to Colin without whose patience this would not have been possible, and to all my other angels

To the reader

I have long been fascinated by alternative visions of how things might be. This book attempts to depict some of these visions from a minority and personal point of view. It is about the growth of the self in all its spiralling contradictions. It is about the liberation of the self.

I include poetry because I am aware that all language is a poor medium for describing things of ultimate importance. Poetry has always been for me a medium of liberation .... not a half-way house between prose and silence, but a fullness of both.

To study the Way is to study the self.

To study the self is to forget the self.

To forget the self is to be enlightened by all things.

To be enlightened by all things is to remove the barriers between one's self. and others.

Dogen, 13th century Buddhist teacher.

Prelude

A Ray of Sunlight

Ognuno sta solo sul cuor della terra
trafitto da un raggio di sole
ed è subito sera.[1]*

These lines by Salvatore Quasimodo, the modern Sicilian poet and Nobel prize-winner, have been with me for a number of years now. They have been a focus for meditation; I have set them to music in my mind; I have declaimed them inwardly during country walks. They are beautiful, intensely and quietly passionate. Like a piece of music of which one never tires, they are open to numerous interpretations.

I have loved poetry since my childhood. At school my favourite subjects were French and Latin and in the privacy

*We each stand alone
 on the heart of the earth
 transfixed by a ray of sunlight
 and suddenly it's evening. (My translation - author)

of my room I used to recite large chunks of silver age Latin poets and nineteenth-century French verse. I loved the sounds of the words, their sensuous evocation of people and atmosphere. Above all the words were able to communicate at a deeper level than could the linear explanations of logical prose. I discovered Quasimosdo's poetry when I studied Italian at university and the above poem spoke, as Quakers put it, 'to my condition'.

I remember once visiting an exhibition at the Royal Academy. I passed through rooms filled with grandiose hunting scenes and huge canvasses depicting deeds of mythological heroism. Suddenly I came upon a miniature. It was a simple drawing of a young man's head. I stopped and looked for a long time. It was beautifully drawn and its simplicity had a ring of truth. The other paintings seemed to be hiding from reality behind the layers of their complexity.

This poem by Quasimodo has the same effect on me. The words are simple and carefully chosen. They have the air of finality; but a work of art does not have the last word. The images and feelings the work arouses continue to resonate long after we have left the poem or the painting. These particular lines fitted in with my experience of the world when I first came across them. I should now add that there is something more than the finality of evening and the aloneness of each human being; what that is I do not know, this book is part of my search to discover it.

The ray of sunlight shines through the inevitable solitude of each person. To begin the search we have to face as honestly as we can our own experiences and the whole of our self. I write as a Jew who is gay and who has become a Quaker. That is where I am now. To complicate matters further I acknowledge a great debt to Zen Buddhism and I often find Anglican worship a moving way to God. If all this seems a case of advanced spiritual promiscuity, so be it. The Holy Spirit has wings wide enough to encompass human contradictions.

This exploration of the self, this journey to personal authenticity, is part of the journey towards God. In his *Seeds of Contemplation*, Thomas Merton wrote:

> The problem of sanctity is finding out who I am ... if I never become what I am meant to be, but always remain what I am not, I shall spend my life contradicting myself by being at once something and nothing, a life that wants to live and is dead.[2]

The journey is its own destination. We begin in our solitude. This solitude is not a punishment; it is given to us at birth as part of our uniqueness. Though contemporary culture sees life as a series of problems and confuses solitude with loneliness, our solitude is vital to us because within it we have the possibility of discovering the seeds of our own worth, the potential of our divinity. It is the solitude we have in common that can make for our solidarity, our aloneness can be transformed into communion. Solidarity is not confined to other humans but must extend to the whole of creation. The journey takes place upon the earth and must respect the earth. Our relationship with our environment is not as person to thing but as life with life.

In this book I want to consider what has brought me to the place in which I now am. And on this journey I wish to bow to the angels who have crossed my path. Angels rarely wear wings. They rarely look angelic. Their messages often need decoding or else take years to make sense. Sometimes I am tempted to throw them out of the house, because their messages seem so contrary to what nice angels should be bearing. But that was always the way with angels.

Part 1
Names that are given

1 Minorities and the Self

What matters is not that we are alone, but what we do with our solitude.

I should like to take the story of the Garden of Eden as a metaphor for early childhood. In this garden all is well. Everything has its place and Adam gives everything its name. Time for Adam does not exist: the garden is an eternity of the present moment. Difference does not exist either: God and Adam reflect each other, both are male and female, both are eternal. But God, foreseeing that an awareness of loneliness might spoil everything for Adam, creates Eve and so makes external what was already within. If Adam is the mirror of God, then there is a fear of aloneness in God also. If God is love then love needs a return of love. But Adam and Eve are soon tempted and disobey God's command not to eat of the tree of the knowledge of good and evil. Adam and his partner eat the fruit. This does not lead at first to death as Eve had told the serpent it would; it leads to self awareness.

Before they ate the fruit, their existence was static, everything was taken for granted. They lived in a world of statements. Now they have knowledge and their eyes are open. God speaks to them in questions. They hear a voice and know that it is a challenge: 'Where are you?' is the first question that God puts to all people. When I was a child my Hebrew teacher told me that that was the first and the eternal question that God puts to all of us. Neither the question nor the answer are ever final. So now the eyes of these children of creation are open to their nakedness and their ears open to questioning. Though God takes pity and makes them a tunic out of skins, these two people, the ancestors of our solitudes, know that they must go abroad and leave Eden.

From the other side of the gates where angels stand with flaming swords, we, like Adam and Eve, look back in bewilderment. Soon we sentimentalise the hidden garden of childhood, full of the flowers of innocence and the fruit trees of carefree pleasure — those of us, that is, for whom childhood was not a place of the poisonous serpents of hunger, abuse, and violence. For in reality Eden is a place of potential loneliness whose trees threaten death. The difference between Eden and the world lies in our having our eyes open. To try to close them after leaving Eden is no solution. The angels are still there with their swords. To try to return would be the way to the death of the spirit, for this would be a rejection of all subsequent experience. The awareness of solitude may become so great that we feel totally alienated. And so we look for a more protective authority figure to replace the one who drove us out, one and who will make everything right again. This new god may be an omnipotent father, an all-providing mother, the party, the clan, religion; anything as long as we do not have to look at the frightening silence where the living image of God still broods within each of us.

Eden is the first stage of consciousness. It is full of contradictions but like children we do not notice them or do not see their incompatibility. We are dependent on what the grown-ups, 'the people who know', tell us. This stage however is unstable. We soon begin to use our own eyes. We see the clay of our parents' feet. We may rage, rebel, reject authority. Or else we look for something to cover up the clay. We try to protect those who we feel have betrayed us. We close our eyes because the pain of keeping them open is too great to bear. We look again for the comforts of Eden. Anthony Bloom in his *Meditations on a Theme* also describes this as a choice between life and death;

> To be sure to go through life unscathed, we hide in an ivory tower, close our minds, stifle our imagination, harden our heart, make ourselves as insensitive as we can, because, above all, we are afraid of being hurt, wounded — and we become at best like those little marine organisms that, frail and vulnerable, secrete a hard shell that will keep them safe, but also imprison them in an unyielding coral armour that slowly kills them. Security and death are correlative. Only risk and insecurity are compatible with life.[3]

So we have to go forward, eyes open, with all our loneliness, insecurities, struggling with the demons and angels we meet on our journey. And yet these demons and angels have many gifts to offer.

The Development of consciousness

The development of consciousness may be divided into three stages (although this division is one of convenience rather than an attempt at scientific or psychological precision). Eden, which I call the thesis, or the state full of

11

contradictions. This is the stage where we accept the names and identities that others give to us as part of the way things are. Then there is the desert, the antithesis, the state of rebellion, the rejection of childhood, where we may reject these names and try out new ones for ourselves. Thirdly there is the promised land of fulfilment of the self, synthesis, the resolution of contradictions. At each stage we can stop and falter. Some people prefer their Eden-like ignorance, the day-to-day survival, which T. S. Eliot calls 'living and partly living'. Some remain rebels in the desert. They define themselves by the negative, they take pride in the attitude of opposition. Others can see the contradictions but feel strong enough to take them on board and live with them in a dynamic tension. They try to remain open to new experiences. Even the latter stage is not final. New painful contradictions may arise and we may not wish to notice them. We are then hurt when a new generation of travellers points out that what we thought was our house of freedom in the promised land is really the hard shell of our self-made security. The journey never ends.

This process is not confined to individuals. Whole groups may go through these stages. I wish to consider those groups of which I am part—those minorities which have helped me to gain an insight into myself. I am aware that we are all a minority of one, but it is natural that people should look for groups of others like themselves who affirm them in a world which is not, on the whole, affirmative. As a child I was asked by my headmaster why we Jews always stuck together. We lived in Jewish areas, had our lunch together, hated organised sports together. We caused our own problems, he hinted. Yet as Jewish children we often felt insecure in a world where to be Jewish was to be different and hence to be threatened.

12

I do not believe that the 'Jewish problem' is a simply a problem of the Jews, nor is the 'gay problem', nor any minority problem, the problem simply of the people concerned. They are the problems that the whole of the wider community finds when it has to cope with anything different. To return to my biblical metaphor (and it is a metaphor only, I am using the Genesis story as a poem not as history), Eden was at first no threat to Adam and Eve. Everything had its place and all was well until their eyes were forced open. Then they saw they were apart from the world around them. The idea of 'otherness' had been born. When we become aware of the other, the new, the different, our own identity is threatened. We then project back onto the other our own difficulties—our fears about who we are becomes 'their problems'. We begin to define ourselves in contradistinction to others. The message that anyone who finds him, or herself, in a minority group soon hears may be stated like this:

> you are not like us
>
> we are the normal ones
> you are the deviant
> we are the powerful ones
> you have no real power;
> if you try to be like us
> we may accept you
> -but that depends on us
> and on how deviant you are.
> Don't ever say your way is as valid as ours
> we might get worried
> we might attack
> in fact—*We are who we are*
> *because you are not who we are.*

It is not surprising then that minority groups stick together. The need to belong is extremely powerful. Belonging confers identity. As a young man I felt extremely isolated, and even to associate with others who were isolated was very difficult. Mistrust often led me to an arrogant self-assertiveness which in turn walled me up in my private world. When I did reach out to others it was sometimes like a collision of bricks. At other times it was like being at the mercy of a hurricane and the shutters went up again.

Overcoming the first obstacle and finally meeting other members of minorities, led me to wish to remain firmly in the ghetto—at first the literal ghetto of the Jewish community and then, when I could find it, the gay ghetto. I can still sympathise with those who carry their ghetto on their backs like a posse of snails. I understand the separatists who express vociferously their need for time and space to reclaim their power and dignity. And yet for me authenticity involves accepting creatively my uniqueness and making of the uniqueness a gift to the larger community. Each person and group has a diversity of gifts to offer to the solidarity of the whole of humanity. If 'black is beautiful' and 'gay is beautiful', it is because we are all beautiful. That is often a very painful discovery, because it goes against everything that we have been taught in a world where, to fit in, we are told to be less of ourselves; in a religious tradition, where we are told that the less we are ourselves, the more we find of God.

What is a minority?

The *Shorter Oxford Dictionary* defines 'minority' as 'the condition or fact of being smaller, inferior, or subordinate'.

The question of numbers leads directly to the issue of power. A minority can only exist in relationship to a majority. It is defined by its relative powerlessness. Some smaller groups do not come into this definition. If you looked at the notice-board of a college offering minority studies you might find on the list: black studies, women's studies, gay studies, and so on, but not red-haired or left-handed people's studies. Blacks are a minority, but in this country, not globally, so I should define them partly as a geographical minority. Women are not a minority at all in the numerical sense, but are so when it comes to positions of power. Gays are a universal minority, but unlike the first two groups are largely invisible as a minority. Red hair is a socially neutral factor in our society. In medieval Christian Europe red was regarded as the colour of the hair of Judas Iscariot and therefore very unfortunate and no doubt some people were taunted because of this coincidence. But I am not aware the red-haired people ever came together for protection, nor that they saw themselves as less powerful or inferior. Left-handed people used to suffer at school because of unsympathetic teachers but again I am not aware of the 'league for the support of the left-handed'. In other words what is important is the position that any group has in the particular society in which it exists. A 'group' is any amalgam of people who happen to have characteristics in common; a 'minority' is a group which has socially relevant characteristics in common, which in some ways set them at odds with others in society. These characteristics are often seen to be not only different, but also inferior. Men are numerically a minority, but only numerically.

Power is the ability to define reality for others. This power is experienced through the language society uses, through the legal and political systems, in the way it conveys standards of ethics, through the way in which it orders its priorities. Society is all of us and most of us consciously or unconsciously accept the dominant values. These come to us through our schooling, the newspapers we read, the adverts we glance at, the television we spend much of our time watching, even the sports we play and the way we spend our holidays. If in small ways we are unconventional, no matter, the system can accept that; it is when we really challenge the fundamental values around us that the problem arises. Minorities simply by existing and demanding equality are a threat. When women talk of inequality of power, they are accused of being at best unfeminine and at worst unnatural—but this leads to the question of who defines femininity and nature. When gays talk of oppression, they are called subversive and in some countries are imprisoned. They are sometimes even murdered. 'Why can't a woman be more like a man?' asks the professor in *My Fair Lady*. 'We don't mind them as long as they don't flaunt themselves', comments the moderate newspaper editor. That is the liberal response: accept the role we give you and all will be well. Above all, don't protest too much. Stridency isn't in good taste!

The social norm

In his *Stigma*, Erving Goffman, writes:

> ... in an important sense there is only one complete unblushing male in America: a young, married, white, urban, northern, heterosexual, Protestant father of college education, fully employed, of good complexion, weight and height and a recent record in sports. Every American male tends to look out upon the world from

this perspective, thus constituting one sense in which one can speak of a common value system in America.[4]

Such a person must be relatively hard to find! Yet advertising is directed at him; mortgages are arranged for him; business is based upon his assumptions; newspapers appeal to his standards. However all of us, old, single, divorced, separated, homosexual, bisexual, black, yellow, brown, rural, southern, Catholic, Quaker, non-Christian, mother, children, of little or no education, unemployed, of poor complexion, wrong weight and height, with no record of sport at all, all of us see the adverts, have to live somewhere, need to buy clothes and so on. So we either pretend to conform; or we rebel and claim that our own needs should be taken into account. If we pretend to conform, our anger falls back onto ourselves. We become frustrated and aggressive and may displace our anger in a thousand small ways onto other people around us. We often end up by loathing ourselves in the process. In rebelling, on the other hand, we risk the possibility of being classified at best as difficult and at worst as subversive, especially when we challenge the basic assumptions that underlie the decisions that affect our lives.

Social norms and common values are of course necessary for the survival of any group. What is important, however, is that these values affirm all its members. If survival of the community is based upon the oppression of some of its members, then we have to question this type of survival in the name of a more universal liberation.

How, then, can we be affirmed for being that unique incarnation of God that we each are? We must learn to love ourselves and each other as heterosexual or homosexual, of whatever colour or community we are. To do any less is to insult the God that as Quakers we claim to find in all life. In the exploration of the self, lies the discovery of 'the other' and the beginning of respect for all creation. In this affirmation where we are reclaiming the divine within, there is not only light, but darkness also. Our search for authenticity leads us from solitude to community. On the journey we shall need to reassess some basic assumptions and to reconsider the language we use. This reclaiming of language is like the creation of new life: inevitably there is pain and confusion as well as joy.

Nicosia

How shall a man
cross from cafe to cafe,
a women bear her load
from tree to tree?
Where a road was, is wire
is history charred
and broken like children.

How the city sits
divided between her peoples,
she weeps libations
in the dry season.

..It is not my words
or voice or hands that can reach..
Remember we shared silences
by the quayside, the waves
resounded in our ears.

We held the sky together,
once. Look across now,
let us pull down
the ruin we have built
together. Take hold of these
rejected stones and let us dream
together. Rainbows of lovers
ascend and descend
as the muezzin calls out
and angels bear us to heaven.

2 Language: Tyrant or Liberator

'.. all things had their names, given them according to their nature and virtue'[5] George Fox.

'"When I use a word", Humpty Dumpty said, in a rather scornful tone, "it means just what I choose it to mean—neither more or less".
"The question is," said Alice, "whether you can make words mean so many different things,"
"The question is," said Humpty Dumpty, "which is to be master—that's all".'[6] Lewis Carrol.

In the beginning was the Word and the Word became flesh and dwelt amongst us. It is through the word that we become real to ourselves and to others. The word makes sense of the reality around us. It gives it meaning and puts it in order. As we grow and as our ways of seeing change, our use of words changes also. As children we accept that things have their names. These names are handed down to us by our parents, our sisters and brothers, the people in the street, in the shop and then in the school and in the books we read. These names embody the value system of our particular group. When we ourselves adopt these names, we are, albeit unconsciously, adopting the same judgements about the world as everyone around us. We are affirming and confirming our membership; we are saying 'I belong here'. The Eskimo child learns that there are many words for snow. It is of course vital for his or her community that people can differentiate between types of snow as their lives and the catching of food depend on it. Aztec children do not have different words for frost, snow, and cold—they use one word for all of these—as such a difference is irrelevant to them. Thus the very words the children use, affirm their membership of the group and its ordering of the world.

As we find ourselves in new circumstances, discover new values for ourselves and join new communities, our language may become more flexible, or may even be transformed. Thus change in language may well bring us into conflict with our original community. One example of this from recent times has been the problems that a number of children from working class families encountered after passing their examinations to the local middle-class dominated grammar school. A number of them became bilingual, using a public language at school and a private one at home and among friends. The successful ones, in the eyes of the school, were those who adopted its codes. Yet the remedial departments of many schools were and are still filled with those children who cannot make the leap from one sub-culture to another. Their language which usually is sufficient to deal with most home circumstances cannot extend to encompass the new ones of the schoolroom where the teacher's use of word and gesture belongs to a different code.

As a young child I learnt that different worlds co-existed. Each one had its own way of expressing things. At home we spoke English, seasoned with Yiddish though no-one actually spoke Yiddish fluently. We associated fluent Yiddish-speaking with the ultra-Orthodox, whose limited English, we noted, was heavily accented (ours of course was accented also, but of course we did not know this, as we spoke Lancashire like everyone else). I do not remember anyone telling me not to use Yiddish expressions at school. That was something we learned there with Christmas holidays and music lessons and other non-Jewish, non-working class activities.

At the age of eight or nine I began attending Hebrew classes after school in the evening. Here I was introduced to Hebrew as a holy, therefore unspoken, language, I was taught that those Zionists who believed that all Jews should live in Israel and speak Hebrew all the time were wicked because they were jumping the gun about the coming of the Messiah and profaning the holy language by using it outside of prayer with their heads uncovered. So as a child I knew there were different languages and that each language represented a different moral code or outlook on the world. I also learned that the reformed and, worst of all, liberal Jews would burn in Hell because they knew no Yiddish and had expelled Hebrew from the synagogues. (I later discovered that they did use Hebrew, but I had given up consigning people to hell, so that did not matter).

All this was rather confusing as my parents in fact were only nominally Orthodox, spoke little Yiddish, knew no Hebrew, were vaguely Zionist, and thought too much religion was good for nobody. 'Goyim', as we called non-

Jews, were out of the picture, beyond the pale. I was not brought up to think of myself as English. Nor would I have used the word 'Jew'. I was a 'Yid'. 'Jew' was the word that goyim used about us. In all this confusion the one thing that I knew was that I wanted to belong somewhere. I needed to identify with one community that would give meaning to my existence. Yet in every group I have sensed two opposing dangers: on the one hand, the group's desire to dominate and gain the total adherence of all of its members and on the other, so to split itself from the community around as to become a self-righteous sect. Linguistically, it has tried to enforce its particular jargon on its followers or has presumed that unless you use its approved vocabulary you cannot reach the truth. (The group of course defines the truth for you.)

My first rebellion against the Orthodoxy of my childhood was actually over words. We were sitting in the small prayer room of the synagogue where later I was to have my bar-mitzva, my becoming a man at the age of thirteen. My Hebrew teacher was talking about prayer. In prayer he said we express the words which were holy in themselves. Once expressed the words flew up to the holy throne to intercede for us. I remember arguing that the words must express us rather than the other way round. I was used to saying the set prayers three times a day, but I had thought that we were speaking to God in those words. If my rabbi was right, I thought, the words were holier than the people who used them and that could not be right. As I was rather conformist by temperament at that period of my life, my protest must have been a significant revolution, perhaps the beginning of the end as far as my early Judaism was concerned.

I now see this as a conflict between a magical use of language in which the word is essentially holy and effective

24

in itself, (the essentialist position); and a dynamic use of language in which the value of the word depends upon its existence in a particular context, (the existentialist position). The former sees the world in traditional concepts, is likely to accept things as they are, because that is how they have always been, and speaks of reality as divided between the correct and incorrect. The latter sees language as fluid. Appeals to tradition will not be of much use for it is the present speaker and the present context that creates the meaning. Ann Audland, an early Quaker preacher, exemplified this when she claimed that words when not inspired by the Holy Spirit were not true even when on a literal level they seemed to be so. If a priest whose life was not rooted in an intimate experience of God were to say 'The Lord liveth', she claimed, he would be lying—for the truth did not lie in the words but in the spirit behind them. Early Quakerism with its insistence on the here and now inspiration of the word was existentialist: words were not holy unless the context was, and the context depended upon the person who used them. Later Quakerism, though still insisting upon inspiration, soon codified the new dynamic speech patterns. There came into being a Quaker way of speaking and acting, where spontaneity was balanced by correctness and appeals were to 'the traditions of our beloved Society' as though these traditions were touched by magic because of their longevity.

Codes and community

Each group has its own language which reflects the priorities of its users and is sufficient for all its purposes. If we say that a certain language is limited, what we are in fact saying is that it is limited according to our way of thinking. We are judging its values by ours. Children from ethnic minorities learn from a young age that certain values are more highly regarded in the wider community than those they learn at home. Confused by conflicting world views, they are faced with a deceptively simple choice: to conform to home values and find a sense of meaning and belonging there, or to reject them and search for community in the outside world. The latter alternative means adopting the characteristics of the more powerful wider group. You soften your vowels, iron out the foreign or regional intonations, you may even attempt to lighten your skin and straighten your hair.

This process however is a form of mutilation. You cut off your roots, hoping that the new ground will produce new ones. I am not referring here to racial characteristics and inheritance, for beyond the biological I am not sure what these are, and besides talk of 'race' reminds me always of Hitlerism; I am referring to the roots of consciousness in the earliest environment. The choice between the home and the world is a false one. When you have made your choice and rejected the past, something will betray you, because you have betrayed yourself. This has been the lesson that my journey so far has taught me: abundance of life, living fully in the Spirit, is a challenge to all that is false. It demands the acceptance of self, the acceptance of all that one has experienced, however unpleasant; it also leads to a refusal to conform with values, whether of the home or of the wider community, where they violate the integrity of the human being.

A Linguistic Interlude - that isn't one, really

The assumptions of language

In 1887 Dr Lazarus Zamenhof, the Polish Jewish occulist of Warsaw, wrote his first book on Esperanto. Sperare, the root of the word Esperanto, is Latin for 'to hope'. In a century of nationalistic strife and warfare, it was not surprising that people were dreaming of a more hopeful future when communication would be made possible beyond national boundaries and all misunderstandings would die away. This dream appealed all the more to Jews who have always suffered in outbursts of nationalistic xenophobia. If the Quaker William Penn had dreamed of a League of European Princes at the end of the seventeenth century, then Lazarus Zamenhof was the member of another persecuted minority who thought he had the answer to the nationalistic divisions of Europe two centuries later.

The root of Esperanto is Latin with additions from other European languages. Zamenhof was a man of his time and culture. Although Esperanto is spoken by small groups in most countries around the world its structures reflect European thinking; more than this, it reflects male European thinking. The word for father in Esperanto is 'patro'; brother is 'fratro'. 'Patrino' is mother and 'fratrino' is sister. The latter two words depend linguistically on the masculine form. Indeed the 'ino' ending is diminutive, so that the words mean little father and little brother! In a society where women were economically dependent on men it is not surprising that this dependence had a linguistic counterpart.

In an article in *Women's Studies International Quarterly*,

27

Dorothy Smith wrote: 'women have long been excluded from the work of producing the forms of thought and the images and symbols in which thought is expressed and ordered'. This is shown by the fact that masculine forms of words are unmarked forms, that is they are taken to be neutral. Compare the word 'poet' with the word 'poetess', where the first emphasises the artist as creator and so is neutral as regards gender, whereas the second emphasises the artist as woman, even perhaps artist in spite of being woman. Similarly, words which began as both masculine and feminine have taken on specialised meanings when applied to one gender as opposed to the other. The word 'wench' for example originally meant a child of either sex, then it referred only to a female child. By the late sixteenth century it had come to designate a rustic girl or a girl of the working class. It was also used as a term of endearment with, no doubt, tones of sexual harassment and so soon took on overtones of a 'wanton woman'. Significantly it was transplanted across the Atlantic where the word's low social status made it applicable for black female servants. Similarly a comparison of the words 'master' and 'mistress', 'bachelor' and 'spinster' shows how words associated with women have assumed negative associations. Indeed there are over two hundred words for a sexually active woman in English and only about twenty for a sexually active man. Most of the terms referring to men are humorous and light-hearted, as after all the sexual adventures of men are more acceptable socially than are those of women.

Some years ago there was a television series called 'The Ascent of Man', which was accompanied by a book of the same name. One children's class was asked to illustrate the theme. The children drew men walking, men building houses, men fighting, men sowing seeds and so on. No one drew a woman. It was the ascent of man after all! No doubt some people would appeal to grammatical norms: woman is included in man as Eve was when she was a rib. But who defines the grammar? Who appoints the grammarians? Do grammarians seek out the essence of things and discover it to be masculine? Is it a coincidence that most grammarians are and always have been men? The problem is that man cannot be both the whole human race and (less than) half of it.

Speaking of God

When we are describing the world we are describing ourselves, was the great insight of Meister Eckhart. It is a cliche of religious discussion that man has made God in his own image. Perhaps that is why God is most often depicted as a man. For many people the first authority figure is a man, usually a father, and in many societies it is the father who has over the life of his family the same authority as the state has over its citizens. This model of God then is tied in with power as well as with masculinity and so is a very limited model with which to identify. It led Freud to reject the whole idea of God as a father substitute and has certainly made worship a difficult activity for many seekers.

Within both Judaism and Christianity the feminine aspect of the divinity has been so devalued that each morning the devout Jew will thank God that he (sic) has not been born a woman; and the doctrine of the trinity is so formulated that it seems to exclude any idea of the feminine. In the first case, the praying Jew is presumed to be a man as prayer for women is restricted, in Orthodox Judaism, to certain prescribed, usually domestic, circumstances. In the second case however the Holy Spirit is something of an embarrassment to mainstream Christianity as it is difficult to base a hierarchy on the spontaneity of the Spirit. Many of the so-called heretical sects in Christianity have placed great emphasis on the Holy Spirit as the spontaneous subverter of inauthentic systems, blowing where it wills as a gale or a breeze. Significantly, the Holy Spirit is associated with wisdom—Chochma in Hebrew and Sophia in Greek, and both of these are feminine.

Patriarchal authority has problems with the feminine aspect of God. I remember discussing the Lord's/Lady's prayer with a group of Friends during a weekend conference. I had mentioned that I often said, 'Our Father/Mother in heaven' when I settled into the silence of meeting for worship. Someone claimed that as God was not personal there was no need to give him/her/it a gender. Worship for me however is an intensely personal activity and I relate to the other as person to person. Nowadays I tend to use the formula, 'Our God in heaven' which half solves the problem. How do I talk about God? 'I worship him' would be wrong; 'I worship her' would err in the other direction, at least for me. To use the phrase 'him or her' would be to introduce particular doubts about gender into observations about worship. 'Him and her' suggests a duality but it is the closest I can find. 'It' would be inappropriate to describe the quality of worship to which I am referring. Sometimes it is necessary to go beyond the aesthetic, beyond conventional grammar, even beyond outward clarity to the place where language itself reflects the individual's wrestling with truth. Flaubert, the nineteenth century French novelist, likened words to children's rockets pointed at the moon.

Blacks and Quakers

While struggling with the assumptions of sexist language and the invisibility of women in language I was recently confronted by remarks of the late James Bladwin, a black novelist who has made a very strong impact on my development:

> For a black writer in this country to be born into the English language is to realise that the assumptions on which language operates are his (sic) enemy ... I was forced to reconsider similes: as black as sin, as black as night, blackhearted.[8]

Many black people consciously use the word 'black' as opposed to 'coloured', which they find patronising. Just as with the word 'gay' which I shall consider later, a group may well, after years of being given their identity by others, choose a word to define themselves. This is an important stage in their awareness of themselves. It may lead to separatism as an end in itself or may lead through separatism to a new awareness of the value of all groups in a new healthier synthesis. The process can cause great difficulty. When I mentioned the phrase 'the dark side of the self' recently, I was told that there were racist implications in this. I myself grew angry and felt robbed of a particularly expressive phrase. I have never used the words 'dark' or 'light' in terms of colour of skin and so felt this criticism to be unjustified. I can see on the other hand how oppressive it must be to be a member of a group whose attributes are negatively rated. A black child must grow up with a low self-esteem if all around her she hears that black equals bad and ugly. An interesting defiance of this use of language is the black slang 'ugly' to mean good or great. Language also can turn the world upside-down.

As Friends we should be well aware of the power of language. In our early days, we refused to use titles, pointing to the equality of all in the eyes of God to whom alone honour was due and to the fact that no one was master or mistress over others. A linguistic practice that was perhaps even more subversive was the use of 'thee' as singular, (the subject form in northern dialect), although the development of English was to lead to the opposite development of the plural 'you' for each person, irrespective of power or relationship.

George Fox maintained quite correctly that the plural for singular form (you for thou or equivalent) appeared centuries after Jesus of Nazareth. One theory today is that the Latin form 'vos' for the singular 'tu' appeared in the fourth century when there were two emperors; one in Rome and one in Constantinople. The pope after the model of the emperors was addressed by his subordinates by 'vos' and replied in the 'tu' form. This use reflects the relationships of power between them. By the fifteenth century, in Italian literature, Christians used 'tu' to Turks and Jews who replied with 'voi', as the latter were considered inferior.

The bases of power were wealth, age, sex, church, state, army, and family and on each account the lower rank addressed the higher in the plural. At the time of the French Revolution all citizens were called 'tu' as it was understood that language itself would reflect and define the new post-revolutionary world. The fact that in a Quaker meeting a little child can go over to an elderly woman and address her familiarly by her first name, the modern counterpart of the 'thou' form, is a verbal equivalent of the basic Quaker conviction of the universality of God irrespective of all outward differences. It leads to a strong sense of equality in the community.

In his book, *The Informed Heart*, Bruno Bettelheim, noted how in the concentration camps the Nazi guards humiliated middle-class professional Germans by calling them 'du' (the singular familiar form)[9]. German has a highly elaborate courtesy code and great respect for titles. These guards took this verbal humiliation to the extent of actually depriving them of names so that when the prisoners had to refer to themselves, they were to give only their number, group, and sub-group. Each group was to wear a star or triangle. By becoming numbers the prisoners lost all individuality. Their only existence was their being part of a doomed minority.

Purple for Jehovah's Witnesses
Yellow for Jews
Red for politicals
Green for criminals
Pink for homosexuals
Black for anti-socials
Purple for Jehovah's Witnesses
Blue for emigrants
Brown for gypsies.

When the prisoners were told to bury the dead, they were not allowed to refer to 'bodies', they had to talk about the 'shit'—the ultimate in depersonalisation. And yet so great is the strength of the human spirit that when Jews had to wear the yellow star in Nazi occupied countries many other citizens wore the star with pride as a mark of solidarity. Today many gay groups have adopted the pink triangle as an affirmation of the inviolability of the self and its sacredness. When Friends were turning the world upside down in the seventeenth century, they knew well the value of words and signs that challenged the tyranny of established forms.

Colours of the Rainbow

The guards gave out the colours
(I always loved rainbows).
They took out a large knife, cut the rainbow in pieces
and triangles of brightness fell from the sky
fell from the sky like snow on the mud
fell like stars of blood on our heads
in Auschwitz, in Dachau, in Sachsenhausen,
in Treblinka, in Ravensbruck, in Buchenwald.
Stars of yellow for the Jews
patches of red for the politicals
green for the criminals
black for anti-socials
purple for Jehovah's Witnesses
blue for emigrants
brown for gypsies
triangles of pink for homosexuals

flowers of brightest death.
Here, my love, is our bouquet of bitter herbs
gather them, gather them.
We shall reclaim
from the stones and the ditches
from the ovens and the forests
a new patchwork of colour
and cover what remains of our lovers,
our friends, our accomplices,
our sisters, the small children of our dreams.
Next year perhaps, in the city of peace
we shall come to the altar
in garments of multicoloured flame

each with her song
each with his melody
and we shall sing
a new covenant
in fire of yellow red green black purple blue pink.
The letters shall burn deep
into the rock of every broken heart.

Part 2
Names That Are Taken

3 The Gift of being Jewish

A gift is not something that is simply given and received; it is the ability to find grace in all things. As such it never ceases to expand and unfold.

The table is set. Candles offer light. On a special cloth there lie three pieces of unleavened bread, two representing the festival bread in the Temple at Jerusalem, and one extra for the Passover itself. It is a poor bread, a bread baked in haste; there was no time in the flight from Egypt to let the bread rise. Then a roasted shankbone, representing the ancient Passover sacrifice. (Difficult to cope with when you are a vegetarian.) The green of parsley is the green of springtime and new hope; the top part of the horseradish is the bitterness of the slavery in Egypt and of all those enslaved today. On a plate nearby there waits a strange brown-grey mixture of apples, nuts and wine. It is Haroset representing the mortar with which the Israelites built the pyramids and into which were buried young children taken by the guards from the women who formed the slave-gangs. Yet on a plate just near the mortar is the roasted egg, the festival offering, a triumph of life over death. There is a glass of wine for each guest, but one remains untouched, at least by the visible participants. This is Elijah's glass, Elijah the prophet associated with redemption. And there is one chair which remains empty. It is the chair of all those who cannot celebrate this Passover meal, of all those who are not free, for whom this meal of liberation must remain a symbolic ritual.

It has taken me many years to understand something of the gift of being Jewish. It is not something which has come easily to me. As a child I liked the festivals, but was aware that they were yet another thing that made us different from most people. My parents, not being religious, found them another source of discomfort. Food had to be passed by the local Beth Din (court of justice) to ensure that it was suitable for Passover and that always put up the price and we had little money in the home. An aunt used to invite the family to a superb meal and an uncle led the family in the readings and songs. So it was a peculiar mixture of family intimacy, delicious smells of the Jewish kitchen, worries over the cost of food, together with my own childhood fanaticism about how things should be done correctly. For I knew from early childhood that I was going to be a rabbi and I was particularly insistent that the law, as I saw it of course, should be obeyed in every detail. This fanaticism gradually waned, my desire to observe the festivals grew weak, my cynicism grew strong. It is only in the last few years, after having become a Quaker, that I have discovered the rich earthy symbolism of what I spent such a long time rejecting. It was indeed necessary for me to go away so that I could find at a deeper level some of the treasures of the Jewish tradition. The solitude of the search was vital; though it led to much misunderstanding on the part of my family. I have been described as a traitor by one rabbi and though my more distant family is quite tolerant of me, they regard my attachment to Friends as something of a perversity. It is something we pass over in silence. Now when my partner and I celebrate the Seder meal at Passover time, we invite our own family of friends, Quakers, Catholics, Methodists, Jews and strange amalgams of all of these. And there is still the empty chair.

Childhood in Manchester

Eden was a triangle of Cheetham Hill in Manchester. The house we lived in was the apex. The school where I went with my brother was at one foot. Our grandparents' house was at the other. In the school, children of many immigrant families sat side by side. I remember the English children. I regarded them as being posh because they were quite at home in school and stayed in assembly and did not leave early on Friday afternoons in the winter time, though why I should have thought them posh on this account I do not know. Indeed we regarded most other people as posh, since finance was always a problem. Both my parents had to work long hours in factories to make ends meet and then they did not always succeed. I suppose my immediate family thought others were posher because they seemed to belong, were more acceptable, had nice homes. My brother and I when young were not allowed to invite friends home, because our parents did not think the house suitable for guests. They were also very private people and the world was divided between the cosy citadel of the home and the hostile world outside.

We were brought up to think of ourselves as Jewish both religiously and ethnically. Even today I think of myself as British, rather than English, because I have a British pass-

41

port. The matter of the passport was drummed in to me at an early age. It represents to me stability and freedom at the same time. There were also Polish and Ukrainian children at school and I learned very quickly that we were not supposed to play with them because their ancestors had killed ours. In fact my grandmother and grandfather had both fled from Lithuania as children during a period of persecution and pogroms. Later there were Italians and I remember that when I began to learn Italian I would go and visit them to speak the few words of stammering Italian that I had. The Italians were sympathetic as they had no tradition of anti-Semitism.

Being Jewish was a matter of belonging to the group that we called Yidden and which others called Jews. Even when I became very 'frumm', that is religious, I still knew that some people were none the less Jewish even though they never went to the synagogue and perhaps only had the haziest notion of Judaism. In my strict Hebrew school that I attended every evening after junior school from the age of eight or nine we were taught that non-religious Jews were bad Jews, yet they were still Jews to whom we owed solidarity. Suffering was the common lot and suffering led us to stick together.

If I was asked as a child what I believed constituted the Jewish religion I should have answered perhaps: praying three times a day, observing the Sabbath, eating only Kosher food, obeying my father and mother (though in this commandment I was always somewhat remiss), studying the first five books of the Old Testament, and fasting on the right occasions. This is still what constitutes Judaism for many Jews. All these activities are communal ones; they spring from personal commitment and are at the same time the basis of community.

In later years I discovered that the ignorance of Christians about Judaism is overwhelming. Time and time again you hear of the contrast between the two religions as though Judaism is the religion of the Law and Christianity the religion of Love. The harshest injunctions of the Old Testament are quoted, as is Paul's assertion that the Law leads to death whereas faith in Christ leads to life. I shall consider my own commitment to Christianity later, but I must point out at this stage that such an idea is based on a false premise.

Judaism is a way of life. It is the activity of the whole community. Its laws are the regulations for such a grouping. At its best it is the way the whole people brings all aspects of its life under the rule of God. Some of its rules reflect the earliest conditions in which they were formulated; they mirror the requirements of a nomadic, then more settled agricultural people, who later became almost the epitome of the urban commercial classes. The Pharisees, far from being the hypocrites of New Testament fame, were the authorities who tried to reinterpret these regulations in the light of contemporary circumstances. The rabbinic tradition of most of modern Judaism springs from them. When detractors of Judaism refer to the harshness of many of its laws, they are only partly right. The laws may seem harsh in the law book but in practice most of the severe laws were never carried out or else were interpreted metaphorically. The notorious rule of an eye for an eye which sometimes seems to be typical of Old Testament barbarism is in fact a limitation of punishment at a time when any injury was punishable by death; it actually means you shall take no more than an eye for an eye—any more than this was revenge, and revenge was of God not of human beings.

The claims of national exclusivity are often laid against Jews on Old Testament grounds, but it was the rabbis, the spiritual descendants of the Pharisees, who tell the story of God's reproof of the angels after the exodus. The story goes that when the angels saw the delivery of the Hebrews at the Red Sea, they flew up before the divine throne in order to celebrate. God however was angry with them: 'How shall I rejoice that my children, the Israelites, have been saved, when my children, the Egyptians, are drowning'. So in looking at Judaism it is dangerous superficially and out of context to consider the Old Testament laws or the Gospel interpretation. Indeed the Kabbalistic or mystical school of Judaism maintains that the person who takes the biblical text literally is foolish, for it is the hidden law that counts not the one that one simply reads when opening the text.

Of this wiser side of my ancestors' faith I was not aware when I rejected the Jewish religion as a teenager. The learning I had received seemed stale to me. Instead of leading to wisdom and understanding it had become a negative code. Instead of leading to a feeling of unity with the whole world it was leading to a separatism that I felt stifling. The more I read the more I rejected. At the same time I longed for a more real communion with the world around. It would be a communion based on the real me, as I understood it then. The two novelists who influenced me most in the early part of my adolescence were Dostoievsky and James Baldwin, the former with his fearless studies of people in extremis who were trying to discover how far the human being could go in rebellion and yet remain within the ambit of a God of grace; the latter with his fiery concern for honesty and the integrity of passion. All this was heady stuff for a boy of fourteen and fifteen who had never left the purlieus of Cheetham Hill except in his imagination.

My rebellion however led neither to communion nor to the grand deed. It left me more alone than ever. I was no longer at home in the Jewish community, nor did I feel at home among my gentile friends. Indeed I had few friends. Books were my most faithful companions. My adolescence then was a long exercise in loneliness.

The famous story of the Grand Inquisitor in Dostoievsky's *The Brothers Karamazov* was critical in my changing views on religion. The Grand Inquisitor tells Jesus that he must return to the cross because when he walks around the world today he is too much of a challenge to the ordinary churchgoer. The church, the institution, has taken over. Reality is now dealt out in small harmless portions, which is what most of us can just about cope with. Jesus with his revolutionary talk of transformation and forgiveness, suffering and redemption, is too dangerous for contemporary Christianity. I applied this to all religion—it was the opium to take because reality was too harsh, though I still could not give up religion entirely. If it was opium, then without it, I felt the agony of withdrawal.

At the age of eighteen I found myself in a Quaker meeting. But I was soon in the desert again, obsessed with, therefore violently against, the idea of God. It took me many years there before I could begin to come to terms with that other Jew, Joshua of Nazareth, also pupil of the Pharisees.

Although I had rejected the Jewish religion, the question of identity remained with me. I have never consciously or directly suffered personally from anti-Semitism, but I was brought up in a community many of whose members had lost family through the Nazis or during the many other periods of anti-Semitic persecution. The mistrust of gentiles was endemic. At school there were many Jewish children, so we were a very visible minority, and were the butt of various boys who called us names, but I do not recall any physical violence. The one comment I recall from years later that really did hurt me was one I overheard in the house of a friend I had been visiting. The speaker was an old man who had always been kind to me. I had been telling the group earlier that I had become a Quaker. When he thought I had gone, he remarked to the others: 'Quaker or not he'll always be a Jew boy'. The phrase 'Jew boy' I have always found nasty. This comment was hurtful because I was not sure of my own identity and did not wish other people to comment upon it. And it was made by a man I had thought a friend.

Many Jews today do try to hide their Jewishness. There is still an atavistic fear that persecution may break out again at any time and at any place. Sometimes this persecution is internalised, as it is with homosexuals, so that an outside enemy is not need—one does the work for oneself. In his *The Secret Jews*, Joachim Prinz describes the descendents of the Marranos, those Jews who originally remained in Spain and Portugal and outwardly adopted Roman Catholicism after the persecution and expulsion of practising Jews from the Iberian peninsula at the end of the fifteenth century. Secretly these people passed on their faith from generation to generation, until at last very little was remembered of their original religion except the Hebrew name for God and one or two ceremonies. What actually was transmitted was the fact that they were different, even when the days of persecution were over.

The hidden Jews of the Balearic Islands were called 'Chuetas' which means 'swine' possibly from the pots of pork that they kept in front of their doorsteps to prove that they ate pork and therefore could not be Jews. So great was their fear of discovery that for all outward intents and purposes they were devout Roman Catholics and many of them were sculptors of crucifixes. Significantly their Passover was a time of fasting. 'We celebrate it', they said, 'because God has castigated us, knowing that we have become idolaters like the Jews of Egypt'.[10] Circumcision had disappeared because in the eyes of the Inquisition it was an outward sign of Judaism and led to burning at the stake.

In the 1960s, a group of Israelis went over to Majorca to reconvert the Chuetas. A handful of them went to Israel but they could not cope with the open Jewish life they found. A hundred years before this another group of Marranos had emigrated to Jerusalem where they built a synagogue. Every Day of Atonement, a group of the men would leave the synagogue and play at cards at the door. This was a relic from the days when it was necessary to divert the guards of the Inquisition from activities that were taking place inside. This behaviour may be described as neurotic, an extreme response to an imaginary stimulus. Rabbi Hanoch of Alexander wrote: 'The real slavery of Israel in Egypt was that they had learned to endure it'. It is a common reaction among the members of many minorities to adopt the low esteem about themselves that members of the majority hold about them.

The irony of identity for me was that for a long time I actually found it easier to come out as gay than admit to being Jewish. This I think was because slowly and painfully I had created for myself an identity as a gay man; I had not yet come to terms with my Jewishness and so a Jewish identity was imposed upon me from outside. It is only since I have become a Quaker talking to others about their spiritual quest, that I have understood that I cannot go forward unless I seek out for myself the value of past experience. My Jewishness I accept now as part of myself, an identity which I create for myself. To me it means being part of a group of people who have thirsted for God and whose search at its best has illuminated the search of all people. It also means being aware of the tremendous challenge and all too human failure of this people, its wisdom and its pettiness, its divine insights and its intolerance. (It is the very search for justice basic to biblical Judaism that makes me ashamed as a Jew of the Israeli treatment of the Palestinians and to see in the latter my sisters and brothers). One movement within Judaism illustrates these paradoxes for me. And I have only begun to appreciate its insights since becoming a Quaker.

Hasidism

There has always been a mystical strain in Judaism which, as in Roman Catholicism, has sometimes led to conflict between those who touch upon heresy and the more legalistic guardians of orthodoxy. On the one hand the tension is more obvious in Judaism in which God is a transcendent force always beyond human beings; on the other hand Judaism has a certain flexibility in that it has no creed so a mystical interpretation of the Law if grounded on Biblical quotation is quite acceptable. Christian mysticism emphasises the divine within—the movement is inwards; Jewish mysticism, on the whole, leads the mystic out of him- or herself to the power beyond.

This movement towards God is through asceticism or through joyful communion. Both of these find adherents in the Jewish tradition, but the latter is more mainstream and certainly was the basis of the eighteenth-century religious revival in eastern Europe, known as Hasidism.

Israel ben Eliezer (1700-60), later known as the 'Baal Shem Tov', the master of the good name, was the founder of the movement. His basic three ideas were the love of God, the love of Israel, and the love of the Torah. The basis was love, not the fasting and the asceticism of previous generations who had hoped thereby to hasten the end of days. It was an acceptance of the world in all its variety and of the eternal present time where redemption may occur. Martin Buber, a leading Jewish philosopher who was very influenced by Hasidic thought, wrote that the Hasidic concept of the world was one of a world as it was in a particular moment of a person's life; a world ready to be a sacrament, ready to carry out a real act of redemption.

The present moment is the moment of eternity. Here Hasidism is at one with the deepest insights of Christian mysticism. But, unlike mainstream Christianity, Judaism is not suspicious of the body. The Besht, as the Baal Shem Tov was known, told his disciples that the body had to be strong for the worship of the Lord: therefore it must not be weakened. The Besht made religion an activity of daily life and all people could worship from the place where they were in their lives. Everyone had a gift and that was what they could bring to the altar of their meeting with God. Evil was not seen as the opposite of good, but the thwarted will which could be redirected towards God. Prayer was not something to do at fixed times but could be recited when the worshipper was moved. It was not a solemn activity but was accompanied by dance and joy. At the Festival of the Rejoicing of the Law, for example, men danced around the synagogue throwing the holy scrolls the one to the other in sheer jubilation. It must be pointed out that the woman's place was still at home—this was not that revolutionary a movement!

However charismatic the movement, within a generation or so there are signs of institutionalism creeping through and Hasidism is no exception. There were still inspiring leaders but there grew a tradition of handing down authority from father to son, dynastically. The spiritual arteries began to harden. But at its best this movement offered a dynamic and spontaneous relationship between the worshipper and God. Elie Wiesel whose life was almost destroyed in the concentration camps of Nazi Germany and whose struggle with God has been the basis for his writing, wrote of the Hasidic leaders in his *Souls on Fire*. He tells the story that the Besht had always wanted to visit the Holy Land, but he never succeeded. Waiting for him there was Rabbi Haim Ben-Atar. The two men never met. It was said that if they had met, their encounter would have hastened the coming of the Messiah, for

> every real encounter quickens the steps of the Redeemer; let two human beings accept one another and creation will have meaning, the meaning they will have imposed upon it.[11]

Religion then is not the contents of books but the life directed to God, all else is a mere notion as Quakers would say. This sort of life is not comfortable; indeed Buber speaks of the 'holy insecurity' of Hasidism. This joyful acceptance of self and others in the presence of God seems to me one of the most profound lessons that Hasidism has to teach the modern seeker. In this acceptance the solitude of each person becomes the basis of community while still respecting individual differences. The other lesson of Hasidism is however that the greatest insights can be swamped by a new traditionalism and that when one revolution dies, another must begin.

I feel that here the traditional mysticism of Judaism is close to the insights of Quakerism. The sadness for me is that Hasidism in its modern form varies little from the narrowest orthodoxy. Perhaps it is a fervid orthodoxy with a smile and a glass of whisky. It is earthy but often exclusive; evangelical in trying to reconvert less orthodox Jews, but separatist from the world and its problems. It has in some places become obscurantist, obsessed by the minutiae of textual criticism. Having stressed the need to liberate the divine spark, it has tried to bind it more tightly in its authoritarian grip. In spite of all this, its gifts to Judaism and to the world are great. Its tenacity has led it to survive the direst experiences of the gas chambers where many of its finest followers met their deaths.

And yet, and yet. Perhaps because of its need to survive, it has become the shellfish in the simile of Anthony Bloom. Too much exposure to the world would threaten it, so it has hardened its shell around it. Any man or woman, who does not conform, is expelled from its ghetto. It prides itself that there are no deviants in its ranks. It would have thrown me out years ago.

Family Resemblance

*—to Miriam**

There is little resemblance now.
My hair grows grey and my smile
tires with each new vision. Besides,
I have forgotten the street Aramaic
of your lullabies. I'm sure you were darker
than I, spending your days in hot fields,
ekeing out some sort of living,
when the furniture trade was poor.

It must have been expensive
running to Egypt, following legends
from one wonder to another
across the globe. Oh my sister,
I bet you weren't as prim
as the girl who spends her time
doing miracles in the shrine.

I'm sure you must have laughed
as you lit the Sabbath candles.
And when you saw the angel,
you must have raised your hands
in Jewish mock-horror, thinking,
yet another guest to feed
from the diminishing chicken soup.
Miriam, how the humble are exalted,
how the hungry are filled
with the good things from your table.

---

*Miriam, the mother of Joshua of Nazareth. The name in Hebrew means bitter waters.

4 The Gift of being Gay

Gay=Aids=Death screamed a banner held in protest by a righteous parent in north London, complaining against the local borough's attempts to give a positive image of homosexuality.

Jews=Christkiller=Death chanted the devout peasants of eastern Europe as they rushed out of church on Good Friday having heard the Gospel reading. Full of rage, they were determined to teach the Jews a lesson once and for all.

Quaker=Heretic=Death cried the God-fearing Puritans lining the roads of Boston to see Mary Dyer hang like a flag from the high post.

I was sitting on a train travelling from London to Manchester, preparing my notes to write this chapter. Suddenly an almighty rage took hold of me. How could I possibly begin? In the committee meeting where we were discussing my writing this book, I had said that I had not felt any oppression as a gay man. I now realised that this was untrue. I knew that I did not need anyone to oppress me. I had spent most of my life doing that for myself and it was now second nature to me. The fact that I had not recognised this when making the above remark was now to me an indication of just how deeply ingrained this process had become. My anger was and is an anger of outrage. I felt duped and this deceit added further to the wound. I then thought of others whose persecution was both internal and from without. Six million of my people died in concentration camps with a yellow star tatooed upon their hearts. They are mourned, monuments are raised. This will never happen again, say the nations, as they ravage the earth to find money to pour into the manufacture of weapons of mass annihilation. Hundreds of thousands of my people were murdered with a pink triangle engraved upon their hearts. They are unmourned. Silence is their shroud. They are an easy target still for the gutter press, for the police who are encouraged to pile up the number of their convictions to attain promotion, for bigots of all descriptions who want an easy scapegoat on which to project all the complexities of their lives. There are no religious services for these brothers and sisters, hidden all their lives and unheard in their deaths. Now there is the threat of Aids. When it was a problem in this country of gay men only, the talk was of the gay plague and the wrath of God; when it was seen as a threat to the heterosexual population, then something had be done to save lives. Gay men who suffer 'deserved' it, non-gays however were 'innocent' victims. Language once again betrayed the innermost thoughts of those who had so far hidden their feelings under a mask of tolerance.

The feelings expressed here may be difficult for some Quakers. Friends are embarrassed at anger. It is not a kosher sentiment. It gets in the way. It does not emphasize the positive. And so frustration comes out in a thousand other ways. As Quakers we are militant in our pacifism, dogmatic in our openness, we stubbornly stand in the light and do not see the long shadow we cast around us. And we talk of Truth. But truth means facing the facts of our vulnerability and our fears. Being tolerant on the surface and holding to the light within, we are none the less afraid of the gloom around the flame. As a gay man and a Quaker I am also aware of these paradoxes within myself.

I do not remember the first moment that I realised I was attracted to others of my own sex. When I was very young, at junior school, I, who have always hated sports, knew that I wanted to shine at football so that I could be in the team of a boy in the class above me. In those days in Manchester we children had no vocabulary to describe such feelings and it is doubtful that at that age we would have understood them. Of course the world of the child is not one that can easily be categorised. We were not yet adults who could manage experience by putting it into tidy compartments. In addition, the Eden of my childhood was particularly sheltered. I suspect that the playgrounds of many schools today reverberate with vocabulary which my schoolfriends would not have understood. I simply knew from a very early age that I found some people of my own sex physically attractive and that felt perfectly natural. I was not however given any words to help me make sense of these emotions. I am grateful at times for this, as not all the words would have been helpful.

The words soon came however. When I went to grammar school, I fell deeply and passionately in love. I knew I was in love and that love was the 'greatest thing'. Literature told me so; pop music blared the truth out to me; television programmes were full of it. But all the messages were that love only happened between a man and a woman. If you loved someone of the 'opposite' sex you had a real emotion, if you loved someone of the same sex you had 'tendencies'. If you were heterosexual you showed your love, if you were homosexual you kept your dirty feelings to yourself or else you were accused of 'flaunting'. Of course, you were never actually a homosexual, you were a queer, fairy, puff, fruit or if you were being condemned in the name of the God of love you were a pervert or unnatural. The most intimate, life-enhancing feelings in which millions rejoice were precisely the ones which in you were supposed to be the source of shame and guilt. I fell in love at a time when to act upon such emotions was illegal in this country, just as it still is in most countries in the world and as quite a few people in this country would like it to be again today. Not that I would have known how to act. I would have been terrified even if I had the opportunity. I was a very naive young man, but I knew that my emotions were fine because they came from a deep place within, though of course I had been taught they were not 'normal' and so I had no right to express them. In short I did what many people from minorities have done throughout the centuries, I learned to lie. I learned to kill something of the spontaneity of my deepest emotions.

There were no positive role models in the sixties for gay teenagers. There were plenty of negative ones. There were the screaming quean and the butch dike (though not so much the latter, as an unavailable woman is a great threat to the sort of sexist humour that pervades much of popular comedy). These are still the stereotypes that we see on the screen, the butt of comics together with the Paki with a funny accent and the Jew who demands his pound of flesh. These are the roles for the 'Untermenschen', the subhumans of Hitlerian mythology, which is the logical consequence of this way of thinking. I sometimes wonder how so many of us have survived. Perhaps this is one of the consequences of living life in a minority, though some have been killed in the process, and many have been deeply wounded.

During the first conversation in which we ever discussed homosexuality at school, one of the boys maintained with great fervour that all homosexuals should be castrated. When later I told one of my closest friends that I thought I was homosexual, he told me to go and see a psychiatrist. When I 'came out' to a friend at university, he told me to keep a dog if I needed affection. The process of 'coming out' is one of reclaiming the gift of your own reality. It is often however accompanied by a struggle of feelings of self-hatred, engendered by the negative feelings to which I have been referring. In some cases the self-hatred is so powerful that it takes control and may lead to feelings of suicide. Rose Robertson, who founded an organisation called Parents' Enquiry for the parents of homosexual children has said that by 1982, her service was receiving 115 contacts a week. She also declared that over fifty-five percent of the young people contacting her had made some attempt at suicide. The Samaritans also point out that a sizeable proportion of the people who talk to them about suicide are worried about their possible homosexuality. Who needs executioners when the victims are so filled with self-hatred that they perform the task for themselves and much more efficiently?

At home sexual matters were never spoken about. In fact, when any 'modern' plays were shown on television, my mother decided it was time to make a pot of tea and retreated into the kitchen. How English she sometimes was! I was however a voracious reader and the public library was a treasure of information. One day browsing among the shelves I came across a book called something like 'Eros, the Book of Friendship'. I have not been able to trace it since. It was a revelation. Here was an anthology of extracts of European literature from ancient Greek times to the present day and all of them dealt with the sort of emotions that I was feeling. There were others like me! I realised how much I needed people with whom I could identify and whose history reflected mine. It is for this reason that many people from minority groups are today reclaiming their history and culture. They are discovering for example that there were women artists whose achievements were neglected because they were women; lesbians are going beyond man-made heterosexual history to find models for their own integrity; gay men are adding important sections to the biographies of many people, the accounts of whose lives have been mutilated by those who could not or would not or were afraid to respect their subjects' deepest feelings. I cannot remember all the authors I discovered in this library book nor even many of the extracts. I recall Shakespeare's sonnets, poems by Michelangelo, and above all passages from Marcel Proust's *A la Recherche du Temps Perdu*, known in this country as *Remembrance of Time Past*. This vast overwhelming ocean of a novel became the favourite reading of my late teens as Proust dealt with topics which were important to me at that stage of my life: homosexuality, being Jewish in a society that often felt very alien, the nature of art, and the value of human experience.

This discovery that there are others like themselves is of course more difficult for gay and lesbian young people in that unlike Jews or blacks there is at first no counterculture to which they can immediately feel they belong and which can provide them with a model for their development as adults. The lack of solidarity extends to history also. This phenomenon is expressed most beautifully in an article by Wallace Hamilton on *The Secret Life of Horatio Alger*:

> They have taken away our lives, and we have paid for the loss. We have had to see ourselves as radically alone, without historic figures to whom we could turn and who might let us know that to be gay was not merely to be the dirty old man in the park or the women's gym teacher. We have always been there, but we have been invisible. Our American history texts have told a story that utterly ignores Indians, Spaniards, blacks, and women ... similarly, biographies have presented lives as either heterosexual or empty. Look at our family album, at our bachelor cousins and spinster aunts. Where have their lives gone? They have been lost, not because they weren't there, but because we did not know how to see them. It was after all a *family* album. It is time we reclaimed them, for their sake and for our own.[12]

On being gay

Judaism is obsessed with survival and it is made clear to each Jewish boy and girl that they have a duty to get married and produce as many children as possible. The more children, the more happiness might be a Jewish proverb. Indeed Psalm 127 talking of children (especially sons!) is a classic statement of this:

> Like arrows in the hand of a fighting man
> are the sons of a man's youth.
> Happy is the man
> who has his quiver full of them.
> (Man-war-sons-arrows!)

Guilt about sex is not however as much a part of the culture as it is among many Christians. Judaism affirms the body and so is much healthier than a lot of what I should describe as Christian ascetic neurosis. Indeed orthodox Jews are encouraged to make love on the Sabbath as sexual union is seen as the human counterpart to the human-divine encounter. This encounter is of course male to female, and the male is the dominating partner, at least in theory. Alternative relationships could not exist. I remember a sermon given by a rabbi with a degree in psychology who told me there were no Jewish homosexuals. The philosophical consequences of this statement were highly amusing to me. I knew I was homosexual and I was Jewish, so logically I could not exist. If I did not exist, I could not have heard the statement. If I had not heard the statement in the first place, I would not have known that I did not exist..... I took an interest in philosophy from that moment on, but my interest in Judaism began to wane.

In her *Beyond God the Father*, Mary Daly wrote: 'To exist humanly is to name the self, the world and God'.[13] Many if not most of us are capable of relating deeply, even physically, to either sex. It is sad for a child for whom sexuality is problematic anyway to have her or his emotions described simply in terms of sexuality and a negative sexuality at that. To describe these emotions as homo- or bisexual is to put them in too narrow a category. To describe them as perverted or unnatural is to affront the dignity of the person concerned and this misnaming is based upon a total disregard for the given variety of human experience. In rejecting this diversity of humankind each of us is refusing to accept part of ourselves. We cannot be fulfilled while denying others their own full potential. Yet this is precisely what we do when categorising others according to our own limited experiences. Perhaps we could let go for a while and allow each group to name the universe as it wishes so that finally we could each find the synthesis, the coming together of all things, and realise at the same time that all labels are inappropriate.

Homosexual or Gay?

Having stated the need in the end to disregard labels, I now propose to contradict this (but only at one level I hope) by a short discussion about vocabulary. There is for me a difference between being homosexual and being gay. (I choose the word 'gay' on purpose to name one aspect of my own reality. Critics of this particular use of this word rarely condemn pejorative uses of other 'neutral' words flung at minorities throughout the ages. I do not remember for example anyone claiming that the word 'queer' was being misused when applied to sexual nonconformists.) To allow oneself to be classified as 'homosexual' is to allow one's identity to be defined by others; usually doctors, psychiatrists, priests and other 'experts'; it speaks of sexuality unrelated to the whole person; to choose to identify oneself as 'gay' is to create an identity for oneself; it speaks of a way of relating to others as whole human beings. I know women also who prefer to use the word lesbian because they see the word gay as depicting a particularly male life-style. Similarly native Americans have rejected the label Red Indians since it was a name given to them by those very white people who have done their best to destroy their original environment. To be gay is not to allow other people's perceptions to cloud one's own vision. It is a conscious act. It is a revolutionary act.

What then are the gifts of being gay for me? The first

somewhat ambiguous gift lies in the fact that I have not been able to accept ready-made value systems. I have been forced to create my values out of my search for personal truth and to recognise that my awareness of these values has changed as my experience has deepened. This has conferred a peculiar sense of freedom but one which certainly has not lead to complacency. This is Martin Buber's 'holy insecurity' again. Moreover I have had the fortune to be able to test out these freedoms with others on the same journey. This latter gift I have discovered in particular since I have become a Quaker.

Secondly, being gay has enabled me to try to reach beyond the dualistic polarisation of masculinity/femininity. My observations have led me to note that commonly accepted masculine and feminine norms can be destructive to all people. This observation is not an intellectual position but a direct result of my own experiences with men and women. I share this intuition with many gay men and lesbians, though obviously I can really only speak for men who suffer the double bind in this country of not being supposed to show tenderness and affection in public anyway and who then find that it is precisely to other such men that they wish to be affectionate. To feel tenderness for another man, to want to hold and be held by another man, to feel aroused by and in love with another man, is to be subversive of all systems based on an inevitable hostile competitiveness which is supposed to be the mark of the male of the species. It is at this point that the gay movement and the women's movement have a lot in common, in that they point to relationships based on a loving equality beyond stereotypes of gender.

This leads to the third gift which is the perception that just as we can see that masculinity and femininity are not opposites but are mutually redeeming, so we have the vision that all creation is a unity and that each one of us is a microcosm of the whole. In oppressing any one part of it we are oppressing both the whole of it and ourselves. Of course you do not have to be gay to have come to this conclusion, but this vision has come to me through that particular combination of insights which have emerged from my condition as a member of these minorities. For this I am grateful.

This development in my own awareness was a gradual one. At university I knew very few gay people. It was only when I came to London in the early seventies that I heard about a group called the 'Gay Liberation Movement'. It had recently made its way across the Atlantic and it took much of its inspiration from the black civil rights movement. Its rhetoric was revolutionary and spoke in terms of the trans-formation of society by radical gays and lesbians in league with other revolutionary groups. I recall the first time I went along to one of their meetings. It was like a baptism. I was in a room full of gay people! I had visited gay pubs before, but they were scarcely places of solidarity. For the first time I was in a place where gay people called each other brother and sister, if somewhat self-consciously for we were after all middle-class student types. Some came out of their closets, some carried their closets around with them. For me it was a sort of homecoming. It was about this time I met the first man with whom I was to have a deep, long-lasting relationship. Through that relationship I began to see that self-acceptance was only the first stage. The question was now the time-hallowed one of how two people lived together as loving human beings irrespective of orientation.

I had left the Eden of my childhood where I was alone

with my daydreams; I had been in the plain where I had found others who had thought that they were alone and we had formed a sort of tribe in defiance of the rest of the world; the next stage was to draw the circle ever wider. I was taking a deeper interest in Quakerism by this time and my perspectives were becoming broader. Again, this was no linear process. It could not be. Western culture has depicted homosexuality as either a sin, a crime or a sickness—or all at the same time—and will not easily allow those who disagree to forget this. There were and still are quite a few people around who wish to put us firmly back in the closets, in the concentration camps, in prisons, or, if they are nice, onto the psychiatrist's couch where we are supposed to belong. So the most open gay person is aware of hostility towards her or him and is sometimes tempted to want to hide away. The media and most churches do not help.

Many gay people actually see the media and the churches as enemies and I have much sympathy with them. This hostility has made it very difficult for me both as a Jew and as a gay man to understand for example Christian fundamentalism and Roman Catholicism, as both of these are almost enemies by instinct to my way of looking at the world. (Though I admit I have a much greater sympathy now for the latter than for the former, however much I try to understand both of them.) One of the things I have always known about the Quaker Peace Testimony is that it is very important to my faith not because it comes easily, but precisely because I find it so terribly difficult to put into practice. Anger and resentment are two emotions I have still to come to terms with. And yet at the same time there is a great joy in being alive and in the fact that so many have refused to be browbeaten in spite of the pressure upon them to conform to what are for them false ways of living.

Today owing to the prejudices that are coming to the surface again through the Aids scare there is talk of recriminalising homosexual practices and a threat hangs over all the advances that have so painfully been made over the last few years. It has taken a long time for most people to realise that the majority of people with Aids worldwide are heterosexual. Images of disease have long been associated with minority and deviant groups and here was one more convenient example. The banner carried in north London equating homosexuality, Aids, and death is very revealing. It was not saying that in this country at the moment Aids has been most commonly, though not always, caught by homosexuals and that this must be seen as one of the many disasters that have befallen humanity from time immemorial; it was not saying that here was an opportunity for human solidarity and a chance to rediscover the art of loving and caring. That banner was saying homosexuals are diseased in their very nature and ought or deserved to die. That is still the environment in which young people are growing up as confused and as unloved as ever. It is vital therefore that variety as gift be affirmed powerfully and lovingly and that in George Fox's image the ocean of light be seen still to overcome the ocean of darkness.

The journey to the inward temple where all parts of the self are affirmed and transformed on the altar is still a tortuous and tortured one. Rumi, the Sufi poet, wrote that there were thousands of ways of kissing the earth. There are also a thousand ways of loving, each one a human counterpart of the divine-human encounter, each one a healing, each a gift.

Frank's Song

The dead have a pact with us.
Though tombs lie fallow in fields of snow
and our feet break on the dried-out clay,
they wait with us. They bear messages
on days even of great sunlight
when shadows are as short as memories.

And so you return, smiling
in a photograph, a sheepish, unassuming
inward sort of smile. Did it hover
as they drugged you to smother
your rage, your joy, your fear
of finding yourself alone
in another sort of world,
this smile that was your wall, your welcome?

All things touch, the living and the dead.
We smile, we love, we pass.
We embrace with such a force
no warmth remains except
traces of breath in the air,
sweat on the hair,
the smell of fear.

A MINORITY OF ONE

With the prints of our fingertips
we have signed upon the skin of the whole world
vast covenants of loving.
We bear each other
the messages of our flesh and of our silences.

Nothing can divide us now.

(This poem is dedicated to someone who disappeared from our lives some years ago. We knew he had died of Aids only when we saw a photograph of him in a leaflet about the subject.)

5 The Gift of Being a Quaker

Jesus said:
If those who guide your being say to you;
'See the Kingdom is in the sky',
then the birds of the sky will precede you;
if they say to you: 'it is in the sea',
then the fish will precede you.
But the kingdom is within you
and it is without you.
When you have known yourselves
then you will be known,
and you will come to know that you are
the children of the Living God.
But if you do not know yourselves
then you will dwell in poverty,
and it is you who are that poverty.

The Gospel Of Thomas[14]

There are two journeys, the inner and the outer one. They

are not unconnected, though the link between them is not always apparent. It is a commonplace of sociology and psychology to assert that outer events affect and even direct the development of the personality. Yet at the same time there would seem to be some inner directing principle which causes us to respond in particular ways to what happens to us. We do not all respond in similar ways to similar events. There is a circular process; the sort of person we are makes us perceive the world around in a certain way and by the same token the world around us makes us the sort of person we are.

These musings were occasioned by my trying to remember the first references I ever came upon to the Religious Society of Friends, whom I first knew as Quakers. My first journeys, both inner and outer, took place in a Jewish *milieu* where the name of Jesus was never mentioned and where Christians, the 'English', were regarded as, for the most part, hostile. As an adolescent I spent much time at the Central Lending Library in Manchester and to enter it, I had to pass Mount Street Meeting House, which I remember as a forbidding and imposing building with interesting posters outside. But there were many other imposing buildings in Manchester and there was no reason that the Meeting House should have anything to say to me.

The first Quaker I ever met was in a book, Mary Renault's *The Charioteer* . This was the first gay love story that I ever read and the young Quaker was a volunteer at a hospital during the Second World War. I remember this book particularly because it told me that men could love each other and that there could be a happy ending to the tale. It also taught me that some Quakers did alternative service in wartime.

It must have been the publication of *Towards a Quaker*

View of Sex and the reading of Voltaire's *Lettres Philosophiques* for 'A' levels that made these outer references resonate with something inside myself. I had already lost my Jewish faith and yet my belief in God was as firm as ever. Perhaps Voltaire is spinning in his grave at the number of people who have learned about Friends from him and who have actually joined the Society. Voltaire was using Friends as a way of getting at the French authorities who had caused his exile in England in the early eighteenth century. They were a stick with which to beat the French monarchy and the Roman Catholic church. In these letters, Voltaire also mentioned Anglicans, Presbyterians, and Unitarians, but it was the Quakers who made the greatest impact on him. He was almost sympathetic to them against his own will. They kept becoming more than a stick; they were a loving, kind, if eccentric, group of people who took their religion seriously. Even when ironically describing George Fox, Voltaire reveals a warmth towards him.

So one Sunday evening at the age of seventeen or eighteen, I made my way to Mount Street Meeting to experience for myself something of what I had read. I have no memory at all of what happened during the hour. What comes back to me still are the words of an elderly woman Friend after meeting: 'Yes, I am a Quaker, but I'm not sure about the divinity.' I remember being amused at that comment, thinking that when I was a practising Jew, I had never heard anyone say that God was Jewish. I had not considered however that God was a Quaker! Then of course she explained that she was referring to her doubts about the existence of God. I have subsequently concluded that if there were a Quaker God, he or she must really have an identity problem.

I was very taken with this woman, whom I never met

again, at least not to my knowledge. She told me that the larger meeting took place on Sunday mornings and contained more younger people. (When I finally became attached to Friends ten years later I was given the same advice about going to another meeting where there were younger people. I know this advice was very well meant but I worry about the consequences if many meetings tell younger people to go elsewhere!) I began going to meeting on Sunday mornings. But I had to go secretly since my parents would not have approved of my worshipping in such a place. Some years later when my mother came to visit in Southend, she came down to breakfast in a bad mood. 'It's those books,' she said. I immediately thought she was referring to the books I had bought about gay liberation, so I said nothing as we have never discussed the subject. 'All this Christianity', she reproached me, 'I knew I had never brought you up properly.'

It is one of the great sorrows of my life that the two most important areas of my life would have both been completely unintelligible to my parents. Yet their strong love for me, my brother, and each other has taught me that love need not be dependent upon an intellectual sympathy between people, but could be founded on the simple fact of their existence. It is from my parents that I have understood something about the love of God. From them I have learnt something of the nature of grace; a free-flowing bottomless spring of love that pours out because it can do no other. In my ignorance and my wilfulness I hurt my parents often and I was still accepted, an ever prodigal, ever returning son, whose ways must have been at times utterly foreign to them. My father in particular taught me the value of silence. He was a quiet man. He stammered and was not very articulate. When he became emotional, he lost even the little fluency he owned and yet beyond words his genuineness shone through. He was a man of touch and his tears were more powerful than any sermon I have ever listened to.

It was in fact the silence that first drew me to Friends. I had found the repetitive prayers of Judaism empty and if I had doubts about aspects of Christianity, well among Friends no one was forcing me to say anything I did not believe. I enjoyed some of the discussion groups led by the younger Friends, but I was embarrassed that I did not have what seemed to me at the time to be their sophistication. They were all terribly middle-class students and came from south Manchester. I was working class from north Manchester and so from a different tribe. I write this trying to think my way back to my feelings as a very shy and insecure adolescent from a family where no one had been to university. In meeting for worship however I could be myself; I could swim in the silence, in fact I felt completely in my element. In the silence I need not be embarrassed by questions about my background.

One day I was sitting in meeting, thinking something like, 'I wonder what all these good people would think if they knew that I was gay.' At this age I had never met anyone I had known to be gay, though I had experienced romantic love from afar. In fact I was very afraid of going anywhere near the pubs my schoolfriends had joked about or I had read about in the press when yet another police raid had taken place there. Nevertheless I was afraid of what these people might think. My thoughts led me to consider the nature of innocence. Could one keep one's innocence in a world where so much was cruel and evil? How far could one get involved without getting contaminated. I was eighteen and naive, but the question of evil is one that has never left me and it is one that no theologian has ever answered satisfactorily for me. I still find most answers glib and anti-human. Suddenly I found myself on my feet and asked my question about innocence. The silence enfolded my question and though I was shaking, I was glad I had asked it. All at once a woman stood up. 'We are not called to be innocent', she answered, 'we are called to be perfect.' At the end of meeting a Friend came to me to thank me for my words, but it was the retort of the other Friend, as I felt it to be, that remained with me as I left. A few weeks later I walked out of meeting in the middle and it took ten years before I returned seriously to a Quaker meeting house.

If anyone had asked me when going up to Oxford in 1966 what my religious beliefs were, I should have answered, 'I am an atheist'. Agnosticism was too wishy-washy, I did not believe in God any longer and God was going to know it. My question about evil was answered by the argument that if there was any divine meaning behind suffering then the sort of God who could sanction that evil did not deserve to be believed in in the first place. I would have described myself as a passionate humanist who would not cease to protest at the meaninglessness of a world where the innocent could suffer. If there was a purpose, then that purpose was not worth a candle. Besides it seemed to me that much of the suffering in the world was caused precisely by those who preached most noisily the God of love and peace. So I gave up God. Jesus however was another matter.

Jesus, the revolutionary

I cannot remember where I first came upon Jesus. We did not mention him at home and we so avoided reference to 'other gods' at my Hebrew classes that we always called

Christmas 'Xmas'. On one occasion my Hebrew teacher did mention 'Yoshka, that poor misguided man,' and another time on my way to classes I was stopped by a stranger and told that although I was Jewish, I should not forget that Jesus loved me and died for me. I do not think that I was convinced by that encounter. It was only later when I began to read poetry and Russian literature that he came alive to me as a man of passion and rebellion against a false status quo. My relationship with him has grown and changed since that time.

When I left home for university, I found the person of Jesus both fascinating and alluring. He became the poetic metaphor for my own feelings of rebellion, of opposition to the world both as I found it and did not like it. This Jesus was also opposed to the systems which were built so laboriously upon his shoulders. Christianity was to me one of the prevailing ideologies of oppression and its claims to have replaced the cold legalism of Judaism with the warm breath of love I found laughable. I had begun to read the new theology by that time, especially the writings of Tillich, Robinson, and Harry Williams, but did not consider that they made much difference to the average Christian. So poor Yoshka became a sort of model and was more lovable in that having been rejected by his own people, or so I believed then, he was now found too dangerous by his own followers. He had become to them the god on the wall, not the man in the heart.

It was at this time also that I began to read the New Testament. I am privileged never to have read this as a child and never to have been forced to believe every word. I read it with a growing fascination. My linguistic studies had already taught me to be aware of the particular culture in which a word was used and so it was no surprise to me that the words of Jesus were taken from his particular time and referred to ideas current then. Neither did I find it odd that there should be stories of miracles or puzzling that images of kingship should cluster around the person of Jesus; after all I had already read extracts from contemporary Jewish literature and found the same thing there. Jesus was a Jew after all and so were his first followers. What did surprise me was that although Christians knew in theory that he was Jewish, they did not seem to understand the consequences of this. For me all the questions about the miraculous birth and the unique resurrection were not theological statements of belief, but extended metaphors about Jesus' greatness as a man. Besides resurrection was a common enough Jewish belief and messiahship was a long anticipated hope, but neither of these were signs of divinity. Indeed I should have said at this time that to call Jesus God was to lessen him as a human being. He was a spiritual and revolutionary Jewish leader whom Christians and Jews alike were ignoring to their cost. He was the true minority of one against the corrupt world.

But this was all a paradox. As an atheist, of a somewhat ambiguous kind, I should have described myself as a materialist. I was sure that all was explicable in terms of the laws of cause and effect and that life was probably simply the result of chemistry and physiology. The problem was that though my head felt this way, the rest of my being profoundly disagreed. Once or twice I made secret forays into enemy territory. Late one evening I left my room in college and secretly went into the chapel to pray to 'God, if you are there'. God did not answer, at least not in the way I had expected. Another time, I went to the Oxford Christian Union, where I was asked if I was washed in the blood of the Lamb. I came away more of an atheist than ever. Judaism had nothing to say to me at all then. I had left that firmly behind, but Christianity intrigued me, though I was publicly scornful of it.

As an atheist I was also fascinated by theology and theologians. Indeed my friend with whom I was living had trained to be a Baptist minister, though he had not completed his course. He had also given up religious observance, though we were both in touch with two of his friends, one of whom was an Anglican priest and the other had completed his training and was now a minister. One day my friend announced to me that he was going to church. I was rather put out and said condescendingly, 'So you've got religion, have you?' as I turned over the pages of the Sunday paper which was my only form of religious devotion.

A year or so later we were staying with the Baptist minister in Wales. We had attended the chapel service in the morning and Terry had told the few ageing members of the congregation in no uncertain terms that they needed a bit more love in their lives and that like the Pharisees of old they were stiff-necked and they had thanked him and told him they had enjoyed his sermon. After lunch we were sitting in the dining room and Terry decided to put on a record of the Fisherfolk, called 'Celebrate the whole of it'. One song suddenly caught my ear and changed my life. It was a communion song called *Please break this bread, Lord:* by Jodi Page Clarke:

Please break this bread, Lord
Please break this bread,
Bread of your body,
Risen in us.
Pour out your wine, Lord,

Pour out your wine,
Let it flow through us,
To our thirsty world.

We come to eat your bread,
Make us whole,
We come to drink your wine,
Make us wise,
We come in memory of your death,
To give you thanks,
We come to celebrate your life
And give you praise.

Let us be broken, oh Lord,
To feed your sheep,
Let us be poured out, oh Lord,
That men may see
That you are spirit and light
That satisfies,
That you are risen in us
To set men free.[15]

(© 1975 *Celebration*)

These words set me on fire. Somehow everything came together: the brokenness of things and the bread of the world which is made holy by being broken; the fragility of the body, holy in its very vulnerability; the hunger and thirst of people broken by systems and liberated by the spirit and by other people; a divine and physical intoxication when we are made whole. The song brought together the physical, the emotional, the intellectual, and the intuitive sides of myself in a way and with an intensity that I had not experienced before. It was a baptism into a new vision.

My response was a desire to worship. The song was a

song of communion and I felt I had received communion on hearing it. This did not lead me to a church where the communion service was the focus of devotion, but back to the Quakers whom I had rejected some ten years before. It did not disturb me that it was music that had brought me back to religion and that in meeting I would hear no music; nor did I worry that I had not sorted out the theology, I knew Friends would not mind that. What I wanted was to worship, to respond with my whole being to God who was involved in all the suffering of the world and its joys. My silence was full of joy as I began attending meeting at Leigh-on-Sea in Essex. Often I used to cycle back from meeting full of song, my spirits high, my life resting on what I thought to be a firm foundation.

Jesus came to mean more to me now than the noble existentialist revolutionary of my time in the desert. He was now the image of God who lived at a particular time and place, but who was the paradigm of the human life filled with divinity; as such he was both unique and universal. I still would not have thought of him as God, just as he, as a devout Jew would not, but he was, as it were, the human face of God. So I felt I had now been baptised into the Quaker branch of the Christian community. Within nine months of attending I applied for membership and was accepted.

I felt at home among Friends, but it did not take me long to realise that I still felt very uncomfortable in other parts of the Christian church, where in the name of Jesus every knee was to bow to some human authority or inhuman doctrine. I also realised quite soon that initial enthusiasm wanes and that the spiritual life is not made up of moments of divine intoxication. There were times when I disagreed with ministry offered at meeting, when I was amazed at the ignorance of even Friends when it came to Judaism, moments when the whole thing seemed to be a secular debating chamber—this was usually aggravated for me by someone saying 'the whole of life is sacramental, so there is no distinction between the secular and the divine'—which usually made me feel that the sacred had been abolished instead of the secular. I was also intolerant of the traditionalism of Friends—the 'we have done this for three hundred years' syndrome. In addition, as I learned more about the other churches, especially the Anglican and Roman Catholic ones, I realised that a number of Quaker attitudes were in fact separatist, long after the need for protest and separation were necessary. In short I had fallen among human beings!

Slowly I began to realise that we were all seekers and that we all made a mess of things, that we had high ideals and that we fell short of them. It was educational also to discover that even among Friends (that 'even' shows that my regard for Friends remains very high) there were bigots, racists, and people who had made their tradition into a form of idolatry just as in other churches and synagogues. In short being among Quakers made me a little more human. This is one of the gifts for me of being a Quaker in that the Society provides the time and the space for one to discover God and oneself without having to get the theory right and without having to find the appropriate words. It is a wide church, though small in number, and because it contains so many downright individualists, it makes great demands on tolerance.

Soon after joining I began to understand that I had embarked upon a new journey. In these ten years since I became a Friend, I have changed personally as well as theologically. My Quakerism is, I hope, more realistic and better informed.

My present understanding of Quakerism is based on the fact that the God-filled man did walk on this earth but that this Christ quality with which he was imbued is part of the human condition and has been experienced in every culture and historical period, though I should not say that every religion is simply an embodiment of it. Jesus is for me the poetic metaphor of the human-divine encounter. All theological statements about him describe the believer rather than the thing or person believed in. When these statements are taken as objective truth in which we must believe I fear that the resonance of their poetic truth is diminished. They become mere notions, arid and soulless. My worry about an extreme universalist position within Quakerism, one that rejects the Christian tradition as 'unhelpful' (that great putdown word of Friends), is that in rightly putting aside the restrictions of too narrow a Christianity, it can lead to a disembodied and rather vague intellectualism that is uncomfortable with the rich ambiguity of history. My worry about the exclusivist Christian position is that it is too wedded to a particular history and vocabulary. It may confuse the poetic with the literal. In spite of such apparent divergences, the Religious Society of Friends has at its best a balance between the universal and the particular and it has evolved beyond the literalism of some of its earliest advocates. The challenge before it today is how it can use the gift of its distinctive witness without remaining in its ghetto of separatism; how it might open itself to divine grace incarnate in all creation.

I do believe that there is a power which is divine, creative, and loving though we can often only describe it with the images and symbols that rise from our particular experiences and those of our communities. This power is part and parcel of all things, human, animal, indeed of all that lives. Its story is greater than any one cultural version of it and yet it is embodied in all stories in all traditions. It is a power that paradoxically needs the human response. Like us, it is energised by the reciprocity of love. It wills our redemption, longs for us to turn to it. It does not create heaven and hell for us, but allows us to do that for ourselves. Such is the terrible vulnerability of love. This is no theological abstraction, but a matter of relationship. Worship is the word I should use to describe my attitude to this relationship, an attitude in which, in those rare moments when I am fully alive, the whole of my self is open to all that exists in compassion, repentance, thanksgiving, intercession, and praise.

Walsingham:
A love poem

Miriam,
young girl of bitter waters, we have come
far, you and I, from our particular ghettoes
to meet in this soft place where wind
and swans rustle among the late summer foliage.
We have both gone down to Egypt with our broods
of expectations and have been counted
among dour statistics on our return.

Here
they have built you a house and set you
in plaster, ever gazing, ever gracious,
at your first son's first stretching out
to his dark world. Miriam, there must have been
times when you wished him away with other children,
away from the broken pieces of his father's wood.
There must have been days under the fig-tree
when other angels brooded and other girls whispered
and other children built castles of dust
from the dry soil.

Mother,
they have taken you and stilled your yearning,
coated you in cool blue, you, who loved reds
and yellows and emerald tunics. In your name
they have taken your brothers and sisters,
have bled them in the cold marble morning.
have taken your children, have nailed their hopes,
and their fingers, have burned them, and scattered them.

And so we meet
in this unlikely place you have made a home,
daughter of laughter, daughter and sister,
in this lush oasis on our interrupted journey,
a hotel between miracles. On this altar then
I offer you this burning. I cannot wipe away
these tears, you cannot put out this fire.
Together fire and water we touch, we hold the air,
all elements seethe with praise and lamentations.
Miriam, I offer you these wild late-summer flowers
from all the hedgerows of all the lanes
we have passed through together. And for a moment
I stand before you to garland your black Jewish hair
with this makeshift rosary of pain and love.

Lines written at Quarr

There are lives
Shall I open me to them?
The sea glows by my transparent skin.
There is flame
Where my blood is.

Still the bells
Beat out the old self
Beat in the new.
The air ripples my hair
Like a lover.

The sun on warm glass,
Blue, red on cold stone.
Pour me like water
on the blue clay.
Temper me

In the heat of your love.
In me shall grow then
Edens. The sword of angels
Holds in the spirit
Of the God hovering.

Plant the pips
Of new apples
In the depths of my eyes.
Open me with marvels
And I shall praise.

Part 3
Beyond All Names

6 Befriending the Stranger

Within each of us there is another whom we do not know. He speaks to us in dreams and tells us how differently he sees us from how we see ourselves. When we find ourselves in an insolubly difficult situation, this stranger in us can sometimes show us a light which is more suited than anything else to change our attitude fundamentally, namely just that attitude which has led us into the difficult situation.[16]—Carl Jung

As I cycled home from Leigh-on-Sea Meeting I felt that my life was at last on a firm foundation. At that time I saw my future life as a simple continuation of the present. I had my job as a teacher, a relationship that I thought would last; I had a faith that was sure although, or perhaps because, it left space for doubts. Within a few years I had left teaching which had been my vocation for ten years and to which I had never envisaged an alternative, my relationship had broken down (though it was to become later a good and

89

more stable friendship), and I was becoming restive as I grew more acquainted with Quaker traditionalism.

As Quakers, we are very ready to use a few set phrases when asked about our beliefs. It is easy to say that there is 'that of God' in everyone, that 'the whole of life is sacramental'. Of course the greatest truths are the most simple, but when repeated too often and unthinkingly they become cliches, mere truisms behind which we can hide without further reflection. I have long tried to understand what these phrases meant and above all what their practical application was. If there was any truth in them this truth could not be restricted to a theological perspective; it must also have psychological, political and sociological implications.

It was at this time that I met my present partner, Colin. Through him I came to see how limited was my understanding of other people, of mainstream Christianity, and of myself. He was involved in a form of counselling of which I had not heard, Re-evaluation Co-counselling, though I must confess that my experience of psychology outside of Freud and a little Jung was very slight. My journey to make sense of the world was now to take a different path from before. It was the insights of co-counselling, Jungian psychology and Adlerian counselling which were to give me the tools for a deepening understanding of the spiritual quest, and which were to change my priorities from the stage of separatism to that of the search for the coming together of all things in a new synthesis.

Re-evaluation Co-counselling

It was with some anxiety that I accompanied Colin to an introductory evening to Co-counselling down a short flight of steps to the cellar of a large house in west London. It reminded me of the other groups I had investigated when I first came to London some ten or more years before. Each group, I had felt, would provide me with the key to some aspect of personal or social happiness and each had left me, perhaps a little further on in wisdom, but deeply disappointed. My conclusions from them were that there was only the self, the shaft of sunlight, the evening, the inevitable distance between human beings as in Quasimodo's poem.

The room was full. People were sitting on the floor and around the walls. Most of them were in their twenties and thirties, a few younger, a few much older. We were asked to think of a good thing that had happened to us in the preceeding week and one or two of us were asked to go out in front and tell the group how we were feeling. We then had a mini-session: we had to turn to a person near us and speak to them for about five minutes on our feelings about the evening. This other person was not to interrupt us, but give us full and delighted attention while we spoke. After five minutes the roles were reversed. It was quite a strange experience for me to have to listen to someone else for five minutes without uttering a word on my part—not even to commiserate or say 'really' or 'oh dear' or any of those words we usually use to make people think we are really taking in what they say to us. We had to listen with wrapt concentration as one fully dynamic, loving human being to another. That I found at first quite difficult!

I later embarked on a fundamentals course. This was a mixture of theory and practice and lasted for about ten weeks. I then undertook to co-counsel privately with other members of the group once a week for almost a year. These weekly private counselling sessions lasted one and a half hours and were divided into two periods. At each of these sessions two co-counsellors come together, one decides to become the client and the other will become the counsellor for half the time and then they reverse roles, just as in a mini-session. An atmosphere of trust is built up in which each person can bring out her or his feelings about something that is proving distressing at the time. Although Re-evaluation Co-counselling does not aim to be an academic approach to psychology it does operate on a scheme of assumptions about human beings and aims at nothing less than the liberation of individuals from past hurts, to enable them the better to live out their lives in a liberated community.

The model of human beings used in this form of counselling and first set out by Harvey Jackins, in his *The Human Side of Human Beings*, is that all people are highly intelligent, resourceful, spontaneous and adaptable. We can respond freshly and creatively to each new situation and this capacity is only impaired if there is physical damage to the forebrain. The natural way for us to feel is 'zestful', that is full of life and feeling positive about ourselves and others. This, Jackins maintains, is not the situation of the few only, who may be naturally talented, but the lot of all humanity. Obviously when we look around we find that people do not behave that way. The reason for this, he asserts, is that each time we are hurt, physically or emotionally, we cease to think intelligently. Instead then of responding positively to our environment, we begin to respond negatively. The hurt of the experience is stored up inside. Jackins calls these 'feelings of distress' and they are recorded and frozen in the memory. Unless this distress is attended to it begins to form patterns in the mind which hinder flexibility. Each time a similar event occurs we respond not creatively in the present but according to the negative pattern we have stored up in the past. This process is called 'restimulation', it is a process in which we attempt to live out again the old distress experience. We end up by confusing this inadequate way of responding with our real personalities and so begin to think we cannot change.

The first hurts of course are those we receive in our childhood when we are particularly vulnerable. Many of these come from parents who themselves have been hurt and so the patterns are handed down from generation to generation. Small children are less inhibited and they are able to live through their hurts by crying or by other physical emotional responses. This according to Re-evaluation Co-counselling is the way we can all 're-emerge' from our slough of despond. If a child is allowed to respond in this way the hurt is mended. But all too often the parent will try to pretend that the hurt has not taken place, or try to calm the child. The parent will tell him, if it is a him, not to cry, because boys do not cry. Girls are told not to get angry because that is not ladylike and so on. The tears of the child might also restimulate the parent who will then begin to act out of her or his own past experience of hurt. In other words our natural desire to heal ourselves through the emotions of our bodies is thwarted and so the distress is stored inside.

The counsellor is there to provide a safe and loving environment for the client to be able to face again the original distressing events. The client, now an adult, can 'discharge' the emotions forbidden before. In other words its aims are to reverse the negative patterns and to allow people to reclaim their gift as intelligent, loving and hence powerful human beings. It was through this that I learned much about myself and about my anger and also to take pride in being alive—proud of being Jewish and gay—in short to reclaim my own existence without needing to apologise for what I am.

This coming to terms with my anger did not come easily. During one session we had to look at our reactions to the threat of nuclear war. I burst into tears and began to rage and tremble. My anger came from a feeling of impotence. I had become a shy child again but at the same time I was overwhelmed by a sense of injustice. I was furious at world leaders whose finger could push the button at any moment, at those men (and few women) who in the name of progress, religion, truth, the nation, were quite prepared to destroy the earth. And I realised that I loved the world desperately. In the discussion later, we had to think of something we would miss in a global destruction. We were not to feel guilty that it might be a small object, we had permission to say whatever we wanted. I thought of the cats at home, the devastation of the animal world. The anger gradually gave way to a sense of my own power, of what I personally could do. What love could do. Love based on a knowledge of the self, its light and its darkness.

But you cannot live at this peak all the time. Even these wonderful insights had to be integrated with the rest of my discoveries. My association with the Co-counselling group came to an end when, with its meetings and literature and jargon, it began to feel like yet another religious group I had fallen upon. But in my association with it I can say that it had changed my life. It had enabled me to learn to listen, both to the voice within me and the voice in others. That was and is not an easy task.

Co-counselling attracts a number of people from a religious background, but as an activity it is very mistrustful of talk of spirituality. The reasons for this are quite clear: it aims to overcome oppression and religion itself has long been the instrument of oppression. The consequence of this mistrust however has been to split some of its adherents in two using one way of thinking in the sessions and another outside. Re-evaluation Co-counselling itself has split up into factions and has developed a tendency to a certain authoritarianism of approach just like many churches. One line of thinking that I have found more conducive to a spiritual way of thinking is that pursued by Carl Jung, one of the seminal thinkers of this century, who as a pioneer went over the top from time to time and whose thinking in some areas of human liberation was necessarily quite limited—like that of many a genius.

Carl Jung and Alfred Adler

It is with Carl Jung that I feel some sort of synthesis can be made between the psyche and spirituality. Freud dismissed Jung as a mystic, so obviously Jung was on the right lines. What I personally have found so useful in Jung's writings is the idea that the psyche for him is the creative force which aims to integrate the unconscious with the conscious. Jung is popular among many Quakers because he does not consider the unconscious to be the repository of repressed evil and destructive forces. It is the storehouse of drives and forces inherited over the centuries from the collective unconscious of humanity as well of those aspects of the self with which we have not (yet) been able to cope or which have yet to be discovered.

The psyche aims at integration. The healing power is within. When I first read Jung's *Answer to Job*, I was stunned by the sheer bravado of his arguments. The intensity of the dialogue between Job and God is profoundly Jewish. Job, like Jacob in his struggle with the angel, is the hero, indeed becomes the hero through the struggle. It is no longer Job who is brought before the heavenly tribunal, but God is on trial, just as God was found guilty in the death camps of Auschwitz. God is not the higher part of the self, the totally beyond sin, the absolute light, God is part of the process of growth. The struggle for perfection is replaced by the quest for wholeness. For Jung, perfection is the masculine drive which could lead to sterility, for where do the perfect go, after they have reached perfection? Wholeness he considered a feminine drive which, if not focussed, could lead to a lack of purpose. The important thing was to find the balance. And this balance was to be found in God also. For there was darkness in God also, a deep wrath which was the other side of love.

If God was within, I realised that my apprehension of this divine power was related to my own self-awareness. If I could let go of my longing for perfection, there was more room for my relationship with God to grow. God is in a state of becoming, just as I am. Continuous revelation is a revelation of the self and of God, and of the world. This lesson is the perennial one of the mystical tradition to which Jung, Quakers and the Hasidim are heir. Jung has enabled me to see this more clearly than many other writers, but the danger with his writings for me is that they are so speculatively brilliant and seductive that they can take me away from my everyday world of action. As soon as I am so entranced, I hear another voice which tells me to beware of sirens. The air on mountain tops is rare and intoxicating. The plain is calling. And there are other prophets who lead me back to daily life.

In recent years, my job with enquirers about Quakerism, and other areas of my life, have taken me into personal counselling. Religious questions have no frontiers. The search for God is often painful and it may involve a difficult self reassessment. It has been in Adlerian counselling that I have found an approach that I can actually use in my daily life.

When Colin and I read an article about Alfred Adler, another colleague of Freud, we both warmed to his pragmatic, non-metaphysical approach. So off we went to another room where another set of people sat at the feet of another absent master. For Adler, each person is unique, creative and an indivisible whole whose behaviour is logical according to his or her way of looking at the world. This way of looking at the world is based on the whole of their past experiences and how they interpreted them. It depends also on their role in the family as a child and on their goals for the future. The integrated person is the one whose actions add to the sum of social harmony in the surrounding community and in the world around.

All people are striving for significance, which is the meaning of Adler's often misunderstood idea of the superiority complex or the quest for power. If people are acting in an antisocial way, it is because that is the way in which they find their own sense of importance. This antisocial behaviour is described by Adler as 'useless' behaviour. It is necessary to show the client that there are other modes of behaviour which are both more useful to society and allow the individual to feel significant thereby. It must be emphasised that for Adler social norms themselves can be examples of useless behaviour on a corporate level.

To a certain extent, Adler's psychology can be described as a psychology of the will. It maintains that each human being is in charge of his or her own life and that therefore we can change our own behaviour. We can change, when we choose to change. What stops us is fear. We have found a *modus vivendi* and we want to stick to it, lest something worse takes its place. Our strategies have enabled us to survive so far, why risk losing them? These strategies are the way we compensate for past hurts. They help us bear our inadequacies, we would feel exposed without them. The Adlerian counsellor would maintain that if the strategies work, there is no reason at all for change; the danger arises when individuals feel that the past strategies for coping are now getting in the way of their own development. With encouragement, we can be brought to the point where we realise why and how we are using these now useless strategies and armed with this knowledge we are empowered to take charge of our lives and change them.

I am aware that this is a very simplified, if not simplistic, introduction to both Jung and Adler, but these are the aspects of their teaching which have remained with me. They both stress that the healing takes place from within. They are both anti-authoritarian and avoid the division of the world into categories of 'good' and 'bad' as they try to intuit what it is that make us act the way we do. They start where we are and do not try to force us into a mould. In this they have much in common with Friends, although Friends have still a lot to learn about how not to discourage the gifts which are not compatible with what I sometimes feel is the Quaker straightjacket.

Adler writes of the five life tasks: the self, occupation (paid or unpaid work), friendship, intimacy, and the cosmos. Few of us feel that we have the balance sorted out in all these tasks. Indeed I suspect that most of us feel creative in one particular area and not so much in others.... if we feel creative at all. I have so far emphasised the personal individual aspects of development. I should now like finally to consider the bridge between the self and the cosmos. This bridge leads into the sacred circle where the one, the many, and the all, perform the sacred dance.

Magnificat, Requiem

My soul magnifies
(or would magnify),
enlarge upon its hemmed-in space,
bore deep within itself
a larger and larger world
and outwards weave
towards the furthest star
a temple curtain tapestry
sapphire in intensity
emerald in expanse
light in its majesty.

This little thing, my soul,
would open out
to you my lady, you my lord,
at the heart of the rose
within the smallest corpuscle
of this body, bludgeoned and bludgeoning,
to you my lover, my beloved,
encompassing the outmost shell of expanding universe
and all beyond.

For in me you have cast down
the mighty merchant prince,
his ships laden with knowledge,
his peacock mirrors,
and on the stripped bare throne
that totters to east and west
you have set this frightened child
that mewls and pukes

and scratches walls of fear
like a misused cat.

Be it then as you will
that this chaotic army within my skin,
this child at the prince's neck,
this Herod, this emaciated Baptist,
will magnify their God
each in his and her own place.

An aching tenderness
engulfs the world.

7 The Sacred Circle

It was very early on Sunday morning. We had left the house in the dark, had climbed the hill that led to the church and were standing round the crackling flames of the bonfire which were the first flames of Easter. The mourning for the crucifixion was about to be transformed into the gloria of resurrection. On the steps of the church, the priest turned towards the worshippers:

> Eternal God,
> who made this most holy night
> to shine with the brightness of your one true light:
> set us aflame with the fire of your love,
> and bring us to the radiance of your heavenly glory.[17]

A taper lit from the bonfire was then used to light the paschal candle and then we processed into the church for the Easter readings. It being an Anglican church of reasonably high leanings there followed the celebration of mass. Little by little the whole church was illuminated by the candles that each worshipper held, all lit the one from the other as we gave each other light. As we came to the words 'Glory to God in the Highest' the church shook with rattles, triangles, handbells and loud acclaim as finally the period of sadness gave way to new life and then began a series of readings which described God's redemption of the people.

It was at the reading of the crossing of the Red Sea in the book of Exodus that my heart sank:

> the Lord routed the Egyptians in the midst of the sea. The waters returned and covered the chariots and the horsemen and all the host of Pharaoh that had followed them into the sea; not so much as one of them remained.[18]

I have already mentioned one version of this story where God weeps at the plight of the Egyptians, his children, but no one seems to have lamented over the fate of the Egyptian horses, except perhaps Laurence Lerner in an earlier Swarthmore Lecture. There cannot be a partial liberation, there cannot be the saving of one group at the expense of another. The Exodus as at the Passover meal is the meal of liberated creation for there is only one earth and all things upon it are sacred.

The mass, which is a Christian interpretation of the Passover meal, is the process of taking the world of creation as it is, beautiful and spoiled, holy and polluted, and offering it back to God with ourselves who are equally beautiful and spoiled. The drowning horses made me pause because the story being presented was a partial one. If these horses were drowning, then part of creation was being excluded from the process of redemption. The Exodus reading was a narrative from a different time and place. Instead of exemplifying the liberation process, I found it limiting and obtrusive. This is always the problem with relying on set forms of worship to express the deepest aspects of the self. The Eucharist, the act of thanksgiving, should not be limited to any one form or culture, however local its imagery. As in meeting for worship it is the meeting of the whole of creation, where there is no separation; all the diverse elements of worship add to the experience. 'Every creature', wrote Meister Eckhart, 'is a word of God and a book about God' and so must be respected as such. Even the Egyptian horse and its rider rearing and screaming with terror as it sinks beneath the waves.

Human beings suffer from a three-fold alienation: from their bodies, from a sense of human community, and from nature. My experience in trying to make sense of my life in various minority groups is that these alienations are really all one. None of us stands alone on the heart of the earth. Quasimodo in the poem quoted at the beginning of the book is wrong if he means that ultimately each human being stands alone. Our survival as individuals depends upon our seeing ourselves as part of the community of creation. The gift of minority living is that we do not take existing majority norms as truth; we are forced back to our own experiences to consider what is the truth of our own lives. But this would lead to a very partial vision if the only truth for us was that which emerged from that tiny part of the globe on which we found ourselves. That would be the view of the sectarian who dismisses all other truths as falsehoods.

I could not say, in spite of my striving with my inner angels and demons, who probably are the same thing and all part of me, that I feel completely at home in any of the groups in which I have found myself. But the first step on this spiral journey has been for me to accept the givenness of my existence however uncomfortable it has been. My search for community has meant that I have had to (try to) bring the whole of myself to each encounter and yet in every community I have felt the restless stirring in myself that this was only a part of the whole. One of the most difficult challenges confronting me has been the one of dividing the world into two camps, the us and them syndrome that confronts all minorities (and majorities as well for that matter). This dualism which finds expression in the very language we use is divisive and violent and to go beyond it calls for nothing less that the revolution of the heart which is what repentance is about.

The main divisions in this dualistic vision of the world are (and I am grateful to Matthew Fox's *Original Blessing*[19] for his list of polarities):

Male — Female
Straight — Gay
Black — White
Humanity — Nature
Virtue — Vice
Heaven — Hell
Salvation — Damnation
Life — Death
Holy — Profane
Spirit — Matter
Mind — Body
Duty — Pleasure
Supernatural — Natural
Produce — Product
Time — Timeless
Cleric — Lay
Intellect — Emotion

Within — Without
Divine — Human
Human — Animal.

It is not just that we divide the world up in these ways but that we proclaim the superiority of one over the other. We create an inhuman striving, an impossible norm, which denies the gift of being where we are or at least stops us from listening to the Spirit in the here and now of our lives. It makes love conditional on some ideal we can never reach at a time that is always future and therefore cannot exist. It is precisely these divisions that have led to the oppression and self-oppression of minority groups and of women, to the destruction of much of our environment, to the build up of vast and evil nuclear armories and to the identification of religion as the ideology of the powerful. This dualism is blasphemous as it throws creation back in the face of its giver. Quasimodo is right when he writes that we are transfixed by a ray of sunlight, but this ray need not be the dying reflection of a fading sun before the fall of perpetual dark. It can be the gloria of the present moment.

The above list of contrasts is a list of violent deeds. It points to the destructiveness of male-centred materialism with its exploitation of nature, its glorification of disembodied intellect, and its obsession with manipulating and mastering the material environment. It refers also to the life-denying hierarchy of religion with its sanitised heaven in an impossible future with its idealisation of duty and its fear of the human, the natural, the animal. These are the power structures of violence and they create a separation in the heart of all people, including the powerful themselves. They are the power structures of fear, always needing enemies, of whatever minority, real or imagined. They are violent because they make destructive the constructive energies of the universe; the need for love becomes the fear of insecurity; the need to be affirmed becomes the humiliation of the other, and of the stranger within us whom we need to befriend before we can be liberated.

There is another way which goes beyond this fatal dualism. To me it is at the heart of the Quaker insight that there is 'that of God' in everyone, but it is not exclusive to Quakers and many Quakers have even been terrified of its consequences. Other people have expressed it in different ways, peoples, alas, who do not form part of majority thinking and so are usually dismissed, such as Native Americans, feminists, and some of the more enlightened Hasidim. The basic idea of this is that reality is unitary, that is one undivided existence in which all things are in relationship. This is the direction in which modern science itself is pointing and permeates the writing of Fritjof Capra and the New Age thinkers.

In his brilliant *If You See The Buddha On The Road, Kill Him*, Sheldon Kopp wrote, 'for better or for worse, all of that that is not me, is me also.'[20] I am what I am because you are what you are. I am what I am because of everything that I have been, done, said, thought, seen. And not one second can be taken away from me. God has been there also. This can be a terrifying idea. Oh yes, there is so much in retrospect that I should have wanted different. So many paths I could have taken, so much that I should have prefered not to have happened. But happen it did. And in each second of heaven and hell there was a presence with me, in me, suffering and taking pleasure, dying and being reborn.

This Holy Spirit of which each of us is an incarnation is the basis for community or as the Quaker phrase has it we get 'to know each other in that which is eternal' which means our knowledge of each other is based on a profound acceptance of what we really are. Minority groups have often found this, albeit through unfortunate circumstances, as they have reached out to each other for protection. But this community must be life-affirming and turned outwards beyond the immediate needs of its members. James Lovelock expresses this in his Gaia hypothesis:

> the entire range of living matter on Earth, from whales to viruses, and from oaks to algae, could be regarded as constituting a single living entity, capable of manipulating the Earth's atmosphere to suit its overall needs and endowed with faculties and powers far beyond those of its constituent parts.[21]

It is unfortunate that Lovelock should use the word 'manipulate' as this implies the old subject/object dualism, but Lovelock is also stressing the glory of diversity. Unity is not based on uniformity, something that Quakers of old sometimes forgot. We need to value ourselves and the world around as different features of the wonder of creation. To try to lessen the variety is a diminution of each of us. The Gaia hypothesis also states that in this cosmic community our relationships include animals and plant life. And if we as Quakers talk of the whole of life as sacramental, then we must look to the sacredness of all life. An Orthodox Jew has a blessing for all aspects of life. There is a blessing for when it thunders, for a glass of wine, for entering a new house, and so on. Life is blessing. I wonder how much blessing goes on in a Quaker meeting for worship.

It is so sad that the Judeo-Christian traditions for all their talk of God in the world have to a large degree turned their back on the world as a snare and a delusion. The Hasidim talk of sparks of light trapped in a world of matter and that it is up to each of us to liberate these sparks, but today they tend to have merged into guardians of ultra-Orthodoxy. Catholic mystics such as Julian of Norwich speak of mother God and mother Jesus, and that, even though 'sin is behovable', (is part and parcel of the order of things) all will be well; yet her rejoicing in the world is a tiny voice among the more powerful voices of her church. The tradition to which we belong as Quakers also follows the footsteps of the man who at a wedding feast turned water into wine, who used the simple bread and rough wine of his countrypeople to bless the world. A man of sorrows, yes, but a man of joy as well. A man who did not dismiss the world as a place of sin, but who went about healing and making whole. In Buddhist thinking, the Bodhisattva who has earned enlightenment is known as the compassionate one, since he rejects personal salvation, refuses nirvana, and returns to the earth until all are redeemed.

We fear the wine. We are afraid of passion. We have made prudence a virtue and yet talk of living adventurously. This fear I have found also among the Anglicans with whom I worship for all the symbolism of wine and bread. Yet Christianity in the very wide sense that I understand it is profoundly subversive. It takes the body and says: here is God; it takes matter and says: here is spirit. It looks at community and says: here is love. This love is not the bloodless stuff of repressive asceticism, a suspicion of passion. It is passion made compassionate. It is the Holy Spirit as She rejoices and broods, hovering over the ocean of darkness, which is also the ocean of light, sensuality, joy, passion, peace and love.

Hildegard of Bingen, the eleventh century mystic, composer, abbess, painter and prophet, wrote of the greenness of the spiritual life. All of creation she said is 'showered with green refreshment, the vitality to bear fruit'. Those whom she thought spiritually dead she called shrivelled and wilted, but she believed the divine word was 'all greening, all creativity'. The phrase 'green spirituality' has come to mean more and more to me over the last year or so. We live in a wilted and shrivelled up society, of which we are a part. Eden was a green place, but is a childhood haven to which we cannot return. Yet there is a seed in all people since we have all eaten of the fruit of the sacred tree. The tree is no longer set apart in the middle of the garden. It is in our hearts. The wounds we have received as gays, as Jews, as Quakers, as straights, as women, as men, as human beings, have often made us feel that the tree was very broken, would never more bear leaf or fruit. Yet Hildegard hears God speaking to her:

I am the breeze that nurtures all things green,
I encourage blossoms to flourish with ripening fruits.
I am the rain coming from the dew
that causes the grasses to laugh
with the joy of life.[22]

The Tithe Barn at Great Coxwell

The lark punctuates time and space;
arpeggios of affirmation that
sky is sky and sunlight pours
on stone and water, regret and hope alike;
its song, its cry: this is my field
this is and this is....

We leave behind the frosty spring and walk
ears open, eyes open, pores open,
leave behind heaving and striving.
We set out to circumnavigate
this massive place where earth
holds stone, and stone springs forth,
and wood turns on itself to hold up heaven.
One large beam curves a mighty arch,
supports an expectant roof,
holds up a summer sky.
Behind the barn, trees of disparate green
unite on the tender slope.
In front, a millpond clogs with weeds
reflections of passing clouds and years.
It is, it is; the lark intones.
The manor house has seen so many
leave their tithe, so many rise against,
proclaim, 'no tithe to hireling priest',
has seen witch sink in sin,
float in guilt below the pools,
has witnessed old dissensions blaze

and grow obscure.

The photographer muses on beauty
and takes his shot.
An idyll of fields and hills,
stone and pool, one frame
where shadows focus.
The lark arches over time.
The light burns away the barriers.
The white flame takes in the black,
One breath, one blue breath;
this and that are this,
beyond holding out,
beyond all holding,
the stone flows
the water rears up columns
in temples of flame.

References

[1] Salvatore Quasimodo, *Ed E Subito Sera*. Anthology with the same name as the poem. Italy: Mondadori, 1942.

[2] Thomas Merton, *Seeds of Contemplation*. Wheathamstead, Herts: Anthony Clarke, 1961, pp. 25-6.

[3] Anthony Bloom, *Meditations on a Theme*. Oxford: Mowbray, 1972.

[4] Erving Goffman, *Stigma*. Harmondsworth, Middx: Pelican, 1968, p. 153.

[5] George Fox, *Journal*, ed. J. L. Nickalls. London Yearly Meeting. 1952, p. 27.

[6] Lewis Carrol, *Alice through the Looking Glass*. The annotated Alice, Introd. and Notes by Martin Gardner. Harmondsworth, Middx: Penguin 1965, rpt. 1979, p. 269.

[7] Dorothy Smith in *Women's Studies International Quarterly*, Vol. 1, No. 4, 1978, pp. 281-96.

[8] James Baldwin, 'On language, race and the black writer' in *Times*. [Los Angeles, U.S.A.], 29 April 1979, part v, p.1.

[9] Bruno Bettelheim, *The Informed Heart*. Harmondsworth, Middx: Peregrine Books, 1986, p.121.

[10] Joachim Prinz, *The Secret Jews*. London: Vallentine, Mitchell, 1974, p. 181.

[11] Elie Wiesel, *Souls on Fire*. Harmondsworth, Middx: Penguin, 1984, p. 36.

[12] Wallace Hamilton, 'The Secret life of Horatio Alger' in *The View from Christopher Street* ed. M. Denneny. London: Chatto, 1986, p. 253.

[13]Mary Daly, *Beyond God the Father*. London: Women's Press, 1986, p. 8.

[14]*The Gospel of Thomas* presented and published by Hugh McGregor Ross. 1981, Logion 3, Revised version published in 1987.

[15]Jodi Page Clark, 'Please Break this Bread Lord' in *Celebrate the Whole of it*. (Cassette) Sung by Fisherfolk. Celebration Services International Ltd.,

[16]Carl Jung, 'Review of G.R.Heyer: Praktische Seelenheilkunde Zentralblatt for Psychotherapie', IX (1936) 3, pp. 184-7. Quoted in *Psychological Reflections: an anthology of the writings of C. G. Jung*, selected and edited by Jolande Jacobi. London: Routledge, 1971.

[17]*Lent, Holy Week, Easter: Service and Prayers*. (1984) Central Board of Finance of the Church of England, 1986, p. 229.

[18]*Exodus*, 14: 28 (RSV).

[19]Mathew Fox, *Original Blessings*. New Mexico, U.S.A.: Bear, 1983 (cf. appendix B).

[20]Sheldon Kopp, *If you see the Buddha on the Road, Kill Him*. London: Sheldon, 1974, p. 164.

[21]James Lovelock, *Gaia - A new look at life on earth*. London: Oxford University Press, 1982, p. 9.

[22]Hildegard of Bingen, Quoted in *Meditation with Hildegard of Bingen* by Gabriele Uhlein. New Mexico, U.S.A., Bear, 1982, p. 31.